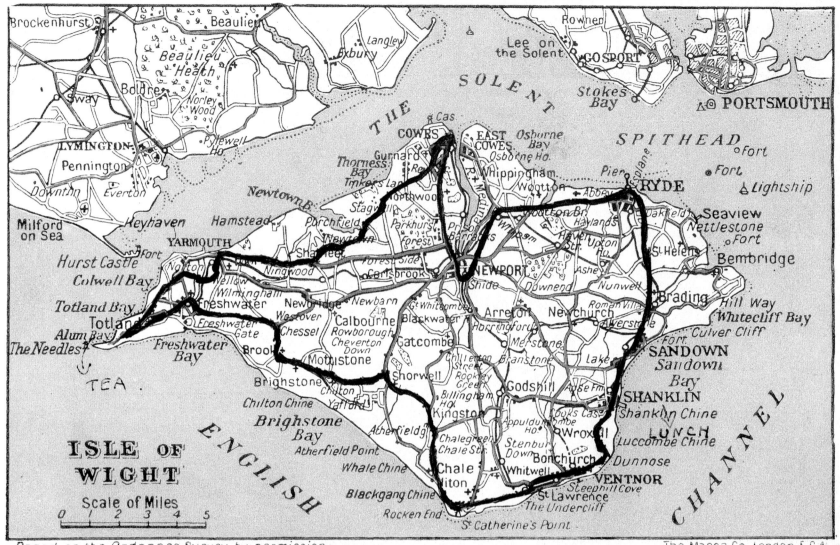

Based on the Ordnance Survey by permission.

The Mappa Co. London, E.C.4

This pre-war promotional map was produced by Fountain Garage Ltd. of Cowes. It shows the clockwise route followed by charabanc operators for "round-the-island" tours. Fountain passengers had lunch at Shanklin and tea at Alum Bay during their whole day 60-mile excursions.

First published 2012
Published by: Chine Publishing
www.chinepublishing.co.uk
Printed by 1010 International Ltd
ISBN: 978-0-9573692-0-7
Copyright: Mark Chessell

Cover photo: Passengers from Carisbrooke and Gunville arrive in St James' Square, Newport. Colson Brothers operated a frequent service on this local route between 1920 and 1939. DL 6210 was a 20-seat Dennis bus that was purchased new by the firm in 1929. This photograph was probably taken around 1936.

Back cover: This beautiful Brannon engraving shows Newport High Street in 1844. A horse-drawn stage coach waits outside the former Bugle Inn, opposite the Isle of Wight County Club building on the corner of St. James' Square.

CONTENTS

INTRODUCTION AND ACKNOWLEDGEMENTS

For more than fifty years local bus services on the Isle of Wight have been provided almost entirely by a single operator. The situation was very different between the First and Second World Wars, however. In those days, when car ownership levels were much lower, many firms competed to carry Islanders and visitors. The number of local bus operators peaked in the late 1920s when there were around twenty five separate enterprises. By 1953, following sixteen business acquisitions by Southern Vectis Omnibus Company Ltd. and various company closures, the only four remaining independent operators were Bartletts *(Luccombe to Shanklin),* Nash *(Ventnor Town service),* Seaview Services *(Seaview to Ryde)* and Shotters *(Newport to Brighstone/ Compton Bay* and *Gunville to Newport).*

In the 1950s and 1960s my family visited the Island frequently to stay with my grandparents in Northwood, travelling by steam train from Ryde Pier Head to Cowes Mill Hill. My initial interest in independent bus operation was kindled by seeing the distinctive Seaview Services' double deck and single deck buses at Ryde Esplanade in their splendid livery of two shades of green and vermillion. Since then I have had a lifelong fascination for the early Isle of Wight operators and their vehicles. During my research I have discovered some intriguing images and information from the nineteenth and twentieth centuries. Curiously much of this relatively recent Island transport history appears to have been largely forgotten.

Numerous books have been written about Isle of Wight railways and Southern Vectis. With one or two notable exceptions, though, there is a real shortage of literature on the independent bus operators and manufacturers that formerly played an important role in the local transport system. I hope that my book will help to fill this perceived gap and that it will appeal both to those interested in local history as well as bus enthusiasts. I have not sought to write a comprehensive account of all the fifty or so independent bus operators. Nor have I covered the work of the many charabanc and coach firms and their popular round-the-Island tours. These are both major subjects that merit detailed illustrated histories in years to come.

Many people encouraged and supported me to write this book. Firstly I am extremely grateful to staff of the Isle of Wight Record Office and Isle of Wight Local Studies Collection who were all very helpful in assisting me to unearth some superb images and key facts from their extensive archives. In particular Isle of Wight Council officers Richard Smout, Sheila Caws, Simon Dear and Sue Oatley gave first class practical assistance. I would also like to thank fellow members of the Isle of Wight County Club, the Omnibus Society and Isle of Wight Bus and Coach Museum for kindly sharing their memories and knowledge of independent operators with me. I obtained excellent detailed information about Isle of Wight Express Motor Syndicate Ltd. from early copies of the Isle of Wight County Press and the Liquid Fuel Engineering Company from the East Cowes Heritage Centre.

Special gratitude is extended to Don Margham, John Wagstaff, Don Vincent, Jim Whiting of Capital Transport, Patrick Hall, Mark Ovenden, Roger Warwick, Alan Oxley, John Golding and Colin Denham for their valuable support. I also wish to thank Robert Biggs, Amy Cosh, Eileen Fallick, Richard Flack, Nigel Flux, Tony Gale, Shelagh Gaylard, Andrew Groves, June Holbrook, Joan Kirkby (nee Wavell), Roland Oliver, Carole Osgood (nee Hunter), Barry Price, Keith Shotter and Graham Squibb and several other Islanders for sharing their personal recollections and photographs of pre-war and immediate post-war bus operation. Most importantly, however, I wish to thank my wife Susan, late father Don and cousin Marilyn Earley who collectively inspired and cajoled me to complete this long term project.

Finally, I wish to put on record my admiration for the various artists, photographers and publishers (including some deceased and others unknown) who took, developed and printed the historic images displayed in this book, sometimes with fairly primitive equipment. Their drawings, photographs and postcards have given me enormous pleasure over the years. I hope that by assembling and presenting this material in a large landscape format their work will be appreciated by a twenty first century audience.

Sutton, June 2012   Mark Chessell

1 THE ORIGINS OF MOTOR BUS SERVICES ON THE ISLE OF WIGHT

During the eighteenth and nineteenth centuries several daily stage coach services were established between the main towns, ports and intermediate villages on the Island. The print above, a copy of which is held by the Isle of Wight Record Office, shows a Henry Mew coach on its route from the Bugle Hotel, High Street, Newport to Ryde via Staplers Road, c. 1830. The team of horses would have been changed at the Sloop Inn, Wootton Bridge.

Until the advent of the mass-produced bicycle and the construction of the Island's railways between 1862 and 1900 Isle of Wight residents were dependent upon various forms of horse-drawn transport (stage coaches, carriages, wagons, etc.) to meet their economic and social travel needs. The quality of roads was generally quite poor and journeys between villages and towns were typically slow and uncomfortable, especially during the winter months.

In 1801 the Isle of Wight was dominantly rural and the total population was just over 22,000. Agriculture provided the largest source of employment and most ordinary people worked long hours on the land for very low wages. Many adults only made occasional shopping or business trips to the main towns of Newport, Ryde and Cowes. Walking was the main way of getting around for most short trips, with journeys on foot of five miles and more being relatively commonplace. There was a much greater availability of key local services in rural areas than there is today. In the early 1800s most villages had their own church, chapel, school, grocer, bakery, butcher, dairy, blacksmith and public house. Some even had their own windmill or watermill and brewery, and communities were much more self-sufficient in terms of producing their own food. The general population were simultaneously less able and had less need to travel long distances. Trips to the mainland were rare for all but the wealthiest people.

From the late eighteenth century onwards enterprising individuals started running carrier services from outlying villages to Newport, the main market town. With their canvas covered wagons, normally pulled by a single horse, carriers supplied an essential means of transport for villagers and their goods. Services invariably operated on market days (Tuesday and Saturday) with some carriers providing daily return journeys on certain busier routes. Carriers established horse stabling arrangements with various Newport inns, with St. Thomas' Square becoming their main 'terminus' and centre of activity. In his book *Put out the flag* Derek Sprake provides a detailed and entertaining account of the incredibly varied work of the Isle of Wight carriers who operated up to 1960.

A good example of a long-established firm in this field was the Shotter family carrier business which was founded in Brighstone in the early nineteenth century. Horse-drawn wagons operated a daily service from Brighstone to St. Thomas' Square, Newport via Shorwell until around 1920 when the firm replaced them with motor vans and motor buses along the same route. In the following photograph a carrier's horse-drawn wagon (possibly owned by the Shotter family) proceeds down Carisbrooke High Street at a steady four miles per hour on its way to Newport.

An eye-witness account of the stage coach and carrier services between Yarmouth and Newport was provided by Edwin Holbrook (1867–1963) in his unpublished memoirs. On leaving school at the age of 14 Holbrook worked at Vittlefields Farm on

This early photograph taken at Shanklin railway station shows 'the Rocket' horse-drawn bus that operated to and from the Royal and Marine Hotels in Ventnor. It was probably taken around 1865, shortly before the new railway line from Ryde was extended to Ventnor.

7

Some inns and 'jobmasters' operated open wagonettes drawn by two, three or four horses. These varied in size and could carry up to 20 adult passengers. They were particularly useful for taking large groups of people to Newport market, to the seaside or to see the horse racing at Ashey. The photo above shows a wagonette with a full load of middle-aged male passengers. It was taken outside the Gem Inn, Ryde, probably around 1890.

Forest Road for four years from 1881 to 1885, commencing work daily at 6am and finishing at 5pm. He was paid just six shillings for his six day working week.

"The carriers passing Vittlefields during the four years that I worked there were Chambers, who drove a four-horse coach from Freshwater, and Simmonds, whose coach was rather smaller and sometimes had only three horses. The late Mr James Blake of Yarmouth, who was a miller and corn dealer, and also the last mayor of Yarmouth, always had an inside seat with Chambers. The passenger accommodation was for eight inside and twelve on top. Mr. Chambers was a tall man with a long grey beard, and he wore a grey top hat. Mr. William Whittington from Yarmouth, and Robert Drake from Wellow were other carriers. Mr Drake's sons carried on the business for many years after the death of their father. Both Whittington and Drake each had a large tilted van. Sometimes Drake drove two horses tandem, the leading horse harnessed with heavy farm chain traces, and on a still day one could hear the traces jingling as the horses trotted a mile away. The leading horse was driven with a pair of plough lines (a thin rope). On the return journey they all left Newport at about 4pm and passed the farm from 4.30pm to 4.40pm. Whittington was always first, as he was very particular to start on time. The carrier serving Newtown and Porchfield was Mr Wallace Greenham from Shalfleet. Some years later he sold the business to Mr. William Smith of Porchfield. During the time I worked at Vittlefields there was a butcher of Newport, Mr. William Dove, who went to Devonshire about once a month to buy fat bullocks, which he sold to the butchers of the Island. They were conveyed to the Island via Lymington to Yarmouth, and were driven on foot from Yarmouth to Newport."

In 1902, following a varied career as a farm labourer, railway construction worker (on the Freshwater, Yarmouth and Newport railway) and landscape gardener Edwin Holbrook fulfilled his ambition of having his own business. He bought the Newtown and Porchfield to Newport carrier service from his brother-in-law Mr. William Smith.

Shortly after her coronation in 1837 Queen Victoria purchased a large estate on the outskirts of East Cowes where her husband Prince Albert designed and built Osborne House. Victoria was very fond of her rural mansion and grounds and spent many happy holidays at Osborne with her beloved husband and young children. This clear royal seal of approval for the Isle of Wight plus the construction of the railways were major factors in encouraging a massive growth in the local population to almost 80,000 people by 1891. Many hotels were built during this period, especially at Ryde, Sandown, Shanklin and Ventnor, to cater for the thousands of people who wished to spend their seaside holidays close to where their queen enjoyed spending much of her leisure time.

The late-nineteenth century was a very profitable period for a wide range of Island businesses catering for day trippers and holidaymakers. Horse-drawn coach and carriage excursions from the ferry ports, main seaside resort towns and railway stations became very popular (e.g. Ryde to various destinations, Ventnor to Blackgang Chine, Yarmouth to Alum Bay and the Needles and Newport to Carisbrooke Castle). Some of the main firms were Young's of Ryde, Vanner's of Ryde, George Mearman of Sandown and Read's Posting Establishment of Holyrood Street, Newport. In addition, many of the larger hotels (e.g. Daish's Hotel, Shanklin and Warburton's Hotel, Newport) ran their own horse-drawn omnibuses and coaches, mainly for collecting their guests from the station and taking them on excursions during their holidays (e.g. to Godshill and Carisbrooke Castle). These firms provided a plentiful supply of employment opportunities for local residents, especially during the summer months.

New horse-drawn vehicles ranging from agricultural carts and wagons to carriages and stage coaches were normally produced by local coachbuilders, such as Harry Margham of Newport or George Mulliss of Ryde. Mechanical, carpentry, upholstery and painting skills were often passed down through several generations of Island families. Vehicles were maintained and repaired by the many village blacksmiths and the coachbuilders. The horses were looked after either by their owners or by firms running livery stables/ jobmaster activities and were shod by local blacksmiths.

A horse-drawn bus makes its way down Newport High Street towards St. James' Square. The picture was probably taken at the end of the nineteenth century and the photographer may have been a passenger on a following vehicle.

The period from 1880 to 1910 witnessed a revolution in road passenger transport in the United Kingdom. Following centuries of dependence on horse-drawn carriages and wagons the late Victorian and Edwardian era was a time of great experimentation and rapid growth of a range of mechanically propelled passenger carrying vehicles. Steam-powered, petrol-engined and battery-driven buses were all designed, manufactured and tested in small numbers in the late 1890s and there followed a few years of developmental and operational competition between the various types of vehicles to determine which would supersede the previously dominant horse drawn transport.

It is not widely known but the Isle of Wight was in the forefront of the manufacture of steam-powered road vehicles in the UK in the 1890s and it also contained a small family firm that was committed to the construction and use of steam powered buses from the turn of the century until the early 1920s.

The East Cowes Heritage Centre booklet *LIFU* records that in 1892 Henry House - a successful American inventor – and his son Henry House Junior set up a firm building liquid fuel steam engines which they fitted into launches at Teddington on Thames. These engines (ranging from 10 horse power to 125 horse power), invented and patented by Henry House, had considerable advantages over coal powered steam engines. Coal took up a lot of space on board a steam boat. To do the same amount of work liquid fuel (petroleum) took up half the space and was cleaner.

Two years later Henry House and Son, with major backing from Sir Thomas Cassell and the English financier Robert Rintoul Symon, established Liquid Fuel Engineering Company (LIFU) on the site of the Columbine shed at East Cowes with all the latest American equipment and techniques. The Houses and their partners chose to relocate their business to East Cowes mainly because Cowes, then as now, was the centre of UK yachting and was therefore the ideal place to demonstrate and sell their innovative and successful launches to wealthy yacht owners of the time. One 35 foot steam powered LIFU launch, the Kariat, survives to this day in good working order with her original LIFU engine. She was purchased in Northern Ireland in 2003 by John Power who brought her back to Cowes.

Soon after it became established in East Cowes, LIFU identified a major new business opportunity. From 1895 it diversified its manufacturing activities and began building a range of steam driven road vehicles running on liquid fuel. Henry House Junior was the manager, his father having returned to America. The Road Traffic Act 1896 withdrew the legal requirement for a man to walk 20 yards in front of a motor vehicle waving a red flag and raised the speed limit to 8 miles per hour, thus creating a major stimulus for the construction and sale of motor vehicles.

During the late 1890s there were several national trials organised for manufacturers of the early motorised commercial vehicles and LIFU was one of the key participants. In 1897 two trials were held, organised by the Royal Agricultural Society and *The Engineer* journal. Only a LIFU lorry turned up to one event, however, while a solitary Leyland presented itself to the other. According to an article in *Old Motor and Vintage Commercial* in June 1965 entitled "*The Trial of Steam*" the Self-propelled Traffic Association subsequently decided to attempt to bring together a representative selection of heavy road motors in 1898. Their idea was to divide entrants into suitable classes and subject them to a set of standard tests on two properly mapped routes in the north west of England. Invitations were sent to about sixty manufacturers. Eventually three firms presented a total of four steam powered vehicles. Leyland entered a four ton wagon, Thornycroft entered a five ton articulated wagon and a two ton wagon and LIFU entered a two ton wagon. The competition rules effectively excluded vehicles with internal combustion engines, whose manufacturers admitted that they could only carry a maximum load of one ton.

There were three Classes in the competition, the main one being for vehicles capable of carrying a load of two tons for a 35 mile circuit on normal roads, starting and finishing in Liverpool. There were two different courses, each of which had to be completed in a clockwise and anti-clockwise direction. The competition was spread over a four day period from Tuesday 24th to Friday 28th May 1898 with the total road test mileage being approximately 140 miles. The three smaller vehicles were each loaded with two tons of bagged gravel plus two official observers who were to note everything that happened on a comprehensive log sheet. There were also several other officials who were based in Liverpool to record any vehicle repairs and adjustments between trials.

From noon on the first day the vehicles were sent off at ten minute intervals and several non-competing cars (mainly Daimler wagonettes) with their interested passengers followed behind at a distance of 100 yards. The articulated Thornycroft led the procession with the LIFU bringing up the rear and dashing away in fine style. Large crowds lined the routes as the vehicles made their way through Liverpool, causing some consternation to the local horse population. First to complete the course was the LIFU wagon, which had an excellent run travelling at a steady 9 miles per hour to 10 miles per hour. It arrived back in Liverpool at 5pm. Next to complete the course was the two ton Thornycroft, which arrived three hours later after having a major mechanical

LIFU's road train, a very early articulated bus, was built at East Cowes and tested on Isle of Wight roads in 1898. The vehicle ran on a service between Cirencester and Fairford in 1898 and 1899. (Drawing by Don Vincent)

problem. The other two vehicles failed to complete the course and limped back to Liverpool for various repairs.

On the second day the LIFU vehicle was again the first to complete the 35 mile road test, although this time it was not without mishap. During the trial the LIFU driver was requested to carry out a brake test, which was completed very successfully. Unfortunately the vehicle braked so sharply that a following spectator vehicle drove into its tail, smashing the tailboard and puncturing the oil tank. Despite this problem the LIFU still managed to complete the last ten miles of the course propelled only by its high pressure cylinder. The small Thornycroft wagon rolled in an hour later, after a better run than it managed the previous day. A further 3 hours later the Leyland completed the course, having broken a road spring and shed a tyre along the way.

The events on days three and four followed a similar pattern, although on Thursday the Leyland was unable to appear, while the articulated Thornycroft took over 10 hours to complete the course. The LIFU was again first to complete the course on both days and on the Friday it made the fastest run of the trial – 4 hours and 9 minutes. Although no prizes were awarded, the LIFU lorry was clearly the fastest and most reliable vehicle during the week.

In 1899 thirty LIFU road vehicles and twenty launches were made, with every part being manufactured in the Columbine yard, including the engines. Everything was built using the most modern machinery, some of it American. An early assembly line system was introduced, and movement of materials reduced to a minimum within the works. There were 12 workshops, from pattern making to foundry, coppersmith to sawmill, joinery to painting and there were up to 220 local craftsmen employed in the business.

All the road vehicles had the same chassis, with different, interchangeable bodies added to meet the owner's requirements. Components were all of regular sizes to facilitate repairs, with spare parts being held in stock by the company. The basic goods van could carry 3 tons of freight and achieve a maximum speed of 9 miles per hour on level roads and 4 miles per hour up hill. The lorry could have sides fitted to safeguard loads and travelled at up to 8 miles per hour and 4 miles per hour up hill. These vehicles could carry 40 gallons of petrol (sufficient for a distance of 50 to 80 miles) and 80 gallons of water (sufficient for a distance of about 25 miles). The Royal Mail and W.H. Smith were major buyers of LIFU vans for service in several cities including London.

A steam-powered 'road train' was produced by LIFU, with goods and parcels being carried in the van and passengers in the rear car. This operated between Cirencester and Fairford in 1898 and 1899 and could achieve reliable speeds of 5 to 8 miles per hour on fairly level roads. Several LIFU steam omnibuses/charabancs were built and some of these vehicles were known to have been operated in Mansfield, Torquay, Edinburgh and Poole at different times during the period from 1898 to 1903. A LIFU steam tram and trailer were supplied to the Portsdown and Horndean Light Railway at some time in the early 1900s. This vehicle was not successful in Portsmouth and was subsequently used as an emergency breakdown vehicle for several years before ending its working life as a booking office outside the Cowplain depot. In addition to its East Cowes works the LIFU company also had offices in 20 Abchurch Lane, London and 24 Rue de la Chaussee D'Antin, Paris. It is believed that LIFU produced three double deck steam powered buses which were exported to an operator in Paris.

The Isle of Wight Record Office has a copy of the manufacturer's original specification and estimate for the 22-seat steam powered charabanc "Pioneer" that was built in East Cowes and supplied to the Mansfield Motor Car Co. Ltd. in 1898.

BODY

To be of the ordinary char-a-banc type but with light top.

To be built of best seasoned wood of a suitable kind, well framed together, screwed and fastened with iron knees and built throughout as light as possible, consistent with the purposes for which it is to be used.

To be painted and lettered according to requirements.

Overall length 18'-2.5"; width extreme over hubs 6'-6"; height to top of funnel from ground 10'-2".

To be fitted with doors between seats on either side, and fitted with slam latches having knob levers on top. Flexible tarpaulin curtains to be fitted along each side and also at back. Seats to be made with bath bottoms and straight backs, except rear seat which is to have solid back to extend same height as backs of other seats. Roof on top of vehicle to extend over driver's seat. Glass protection at front between driver's seat and passengers' compartment. The back to be hinged for letting down and the two back seats to be removable, as verbally arranged.

WHEELS

The hubs to be of either iron or metal, of the latest design, as made by the Liquid Fuel Engineering Company for this class of vehicle.

The spokes to be made of best seasoned English Oak or Hickory.

Felloes of ash and fitted with good solid rubber tyres of a width as prescribed by the Local Government Board for vehicles of this class (3").

AXLES to be made of best faggoted iron with bearings for wheels case hardened. Front axle pivoted with bronze bushed trunnions.

STEERING

A mild steel steering handle connected to pivoted axles by means of suitable steel rods and levers, and so arranged as to have the vehicle under perfect control at all times.

FRAME to be of best channel steel, to which the body will be securely fastened with rubber washers between frame and body.

SPRINGS to be of best spring steel, securely fastened to frame and axles.

ENGINE to be our most suitable compound reversible type, designed especially for motor vehicles (renewable), fitted with piston valves and relief drain cocks, and securely bolted to steel frame. The cranks, cross-heads and connecting rods to run in dust-proof oil cases. Air pressure pump to work direct from engine.

BOILER

To be of our latest type, designed especially for motor vehicles, being a combination of the water tube and smoke tube types, and to be capable of supplying sufficient steam to drive the vehicle at a speed of 10 m.p.h., fully loaded, on ordinary country main roads.

To be fitted with our patent "LIFU" burner, automatically regulated by means of the steam pressure in boiler.

A neat funnel and dome to be fitted as per drawing submitted.

All fittings to be of best Gun Metal; water gauges and blow-down cocks to be asbestos packed.

One Crosby safety valve set at 250lbs. pressure in boiler.

One steam pressure gauge. One air pressure gauge.

Two sets of water-gauge fittings with glass protectors.

One blast pipe and all necessary cocks and connections.

GEARING: The power to be transmitted to the driving shaft by means of steel cut bevel gears running in dust proof oil cases, provided with long white metal bearings, and a mild steel shaft made telescopic to allow for action of springs and unevenness of roads.

The counter-shaft to be fitted with compensating gears to allow for turning curves, having long white metal bearings well lubricated and dust proof, bolted to stiff frame to which springs are fastened. This shaft to be fitted with steel pinions on each end, running in large internal cut gears securely fastened to the spokes of each of the rear wheels.

BRAKES: The reversing of engine acts as a most powerful brake, and ordinarily this method will be found quite sufficient, but in addition to this there will be a powerful emergency brake fitted of our latest design.

PUMPS: One double-acting pump on engines with reduced speed gear capable of supplying boiler when vehicle is running. One Worthington Auxiliary Donkey Pump for filling boiler when engine is at rest, and so arranged that boiler may be filled by hand without use of steam if so desired.

CONDENSER: A thin copper tube condenser, having about 100 square feet of cooling surface, to be fitted on top or roof of vehicle.

TANKS: Two oil tanks to be fitted underneath vehicle, made of stout copper with all necessary fittings and connections of Gun Metal, and capable of holding about 15 to 20 gallons each. Suitable water tanks to be fitted to vehicle underneath driver's seat, capable of holding about 80 gallons, made of stout copper with all necessary fittings and connections.

INJECTOR: A steam injector and 12 feet of hose with proper connections on each end to be fitted to vehicle, and so arranged that water tanks may be filled in a few minutes without the use of pumps or buckets.

LIGHTS: Two powerful lamps to be fitted to dash board, to shew bright white lights ahead, and small red lights behind. One lamp in centre of roof and on funnel to show white light ahead. One small lamp inside so arranged as to throw a reduced light on gauges.

CLOCK: One good brass clock to match air and pressure gauges, to be fitted in a suitable position.

WEIGHT: The weight of vehicle complete, not including weight of fuel and water, not to exceed 40 cwt (2 tons).

SPEED: The vehicle when loaded to be capable of attaining an average speed of 10 m.p.h., on fairly level and good roads, and of climbing grades of 10% at a limited speed of 4 m.p.h. (note: The actual speed allowed by the Local Government Board for vehicles of the above weight is 8 m.p.h.)

TOOLS: An extensive set of tools and accessories, including a motor car horn and copper oil funnel.

GUARANTEE: Vehicle fully guaranteed against any imperfections in material or workmanship for a period of 6 months after delivery.

TRIALS: The official trials to be run at East Cowes, Isle of Wight, during which the Mansfield Motor Car Company's authorised representatives shall be present.

PRICE: The price of the char-a-banc as herein specified will be six hundred pounds, subject to 5% discount for prompt payment. One half to be paid immediately after satisfactory trials at East Cowes. The balance to be paid within 30 days after delivery at Southampton.

DATE OF DELIVERY: As near as possible to 2nd July 1898, to be driven to Mansfield at the customer's expense.

In the late 1890s several complaints were made to the local police about the speeds at which Henry House Junior was driving on East Cowes roads when testing new vehicles. In January 1899 the police set up a speed trap in York Avenue. Two policemen synchronised their watches. One stood by the Queen's gate at Osborne House and the other went down the hill to the bottom, 1,633 yards away. Mr House passed the first policeman at 10.07p.m. and the second policeman at 10.10p.m. His wagonette was advertised as having a maximum speed of 18 miles per hour on flat roads and according to the police it achieved this going down York Avenue (i.e. more than double the legal speed limit).

In the first motoring offence to be prosecuted in the Isle of Wight Mr House was fined £3 with 11 shillings costs. This case generated a large amount of correspondence in the local press with several people praising the police for catching Mr House. There was strong condemnation of "the horseless vehicle". Mr House replied in a letter stating that "motor cars were here to stay and that their numbers would increase on Island roads and that they would become the accepted form of transport." He went on to say that "the opposition on the Island would hasten his departure to the mainland. Customers needed to see the vehicles that he was manufacturing driven at speed and the only place he could do this was on the roads."

LIFU vacated its East Cowes factory in 1900, following the death of its financier R.R. Symon, and all the stock and machinery was sold. The company moved to Poole, then to Southampton by 1910. There were probably three major reasons for the company leaving the Island:-

- The opposition and difficulties of testing new motor vehicles on the roads in East Cowes
- The costs and difficulties of transporting the finished motor vehicles to the mainland
- The death of Mr Symon that led to his executors insisting on the sale of every last bolt and plank of wood at the Columbine yard site

There is no evidence of a LIFU steam bus or charabanc being purchased and operated by any Isle of Wight bus operators. Sadly, not one of the LIFU road vehicles appears to have survived into preservation.

Meanwhile, less than ten miles away, Arthur Herbert Creeth was carrying out independent experiments to build a steam powered vehicle. Arthur Creeth was born in 1845 to William Creeth, the Brighstone blacksmith. From an early age Arthur learned to help his father and elder brother Henry in the smithy on horse shoeing, wrought iron and bicycle repair work. In 1865 together with his brother he built his own quadcycle with rubber tyres, a very advanced type of bicycle at a time when penny farthings were the norm. According to the book *Steam Dreams: The story of an Isle of Wight family 1782 - 1991* by Lilian Creeth there are records of this locally built bicycle being ridden by Arthur in Newport and of it being used subsequently for the delivery of letters in Brighstone by the village postman named Mr Prouten.

For many years Arthur took a keen interest in the development of early steam powered vehicles. He studied accounts of Walter Hancock's steam powered buses in London in the 1830s and 1840s, the Edinburgh steam bus experiments of 1871, etc. and had strong ambitions to build steam buses himself in order to run a regular local road passenger service in the Isle of Wight. Having worked as a smith for the London and South Western Railway in Nine Elms, London for a few years Arthur returned to the Island and married Alice Hookey. After working briefly at Whippingham – where he shod horses for Queen Victoria – he bought out the long established blacksmith's business of John Tharle of Nettlestone in 1872.

The next 30 years were very productive for Arthur Creeth, both domestically and commercially. Between 1872 and 1893 Arthur and Alice had ten children and several of the sons joined their father's expanding blacksmith's business in Nettlestone. Around 1890 (the precise date is unknown) Arthur realised his long-term

LIFU sold a 23-seat steam-powered bus to Thomas Adams of Paignton in 1899. Adams operated a regular service between Paignton and Torquay with the vehicle, named "Progress", for a short period around the turn of the century.

goal of building a small steam powered vehicle in his workshop, a photograph of which is contained in Lilian Creeth's book. This was a neat rubber-tyred tricycle, with two wheels at the front and one wheel at the rear. The driver sat on a raised seat in the middle of the vehicle and there was a seat for one adult passenger in advance of the driver, just above the front wheels. Lilian Creeth states that this vehicle was used to take family members to visit relatives at Brighstone and that it caused a sensation when being driven through Newport.

Arthur Creeth and his sons maintained their interest in steam-powered vehicles in the closing years of the Victorian era but realised that their smithy did not have the capacity to build the steam buses they dearly wanted to operate. Around the turn of the century Arthur approached a number of manufacturers of steam buses with a view to purchasing a chassis and building the bodywork in his Nettlestone smithy. He received vehicle specifications from LIFU, Straker, Thornycroft and Clarkson but none of these appeared to meet his requirements. Then, in late 1908, immediately after the demise of the Isle of Wight Express Motor Syndicate Ltd. bus services (described in chapter 4) Creeth decided to purchase a Gardner-Serpollet steam powered vehicle from the Tower Traction Company factory in York. The brand new chassis was fitted with a 14-seat open-sided charabanc body which was built by Arthur Creeth and his sons in Nettlestone. Its registration number was DL 299.

Creeth commenced running a regular local bus service with this vehicle from Seaview to Ryde via Nettlestone in March 1909. Being steam-powered the bus needed to refill with water quite frequently and this normally took place at the well in the grounds of St. Peter's Church, Seaview and at another well at the Green in Nettlestone. It was more difficult for buses to refill their water tanks in Ryde since furious horse-bus drivers insisted that their horses refused to drink from the troughs in the Esplanade if they had been used to supply water to the steam buses.

A very early bright pink folded card timetable for the new service contained the following information:

SEAVIEW AND RYDE MOTOR CAR SERVICE
TIME TABLE – APRIL 14th 1909
(until further notice)

RYDE PIER and the TOP OF SEAVIEW HILL
Fare 6d, single journey

Week Days
Leaving Seaview 11.15am, 2.00pm, 3.00pm, 4.00pm, 5.00pm, 6.00pm
Leaving Ryde 11.45am, 2.30pm, 3.30pm, 4.30pm, 5.30pm, 6.40pm

Extra journeys by arrangement

'The advertised times will be adhered to as strictly as possible, but the proprietors will not be responsible for any delay arising from any cause whatsoever'

The final rider was added because rival horse-drawn buses who resented the new competition timed their departures so that they left a few minutes before Creeth's steam buses. The horse-buses would then take up position in centre road, making it difficult for the steam buses to pass.

Between 1909 and 1913 A.H. Creeth and Sons bought four Darracq-Serpollet steam buses, including two vehicles registered as OS 41 and DL 502. Some of these were acquired second hand. Spare parts were difficult to obtain and Creeth made and fitted many chassis and bodywork components, including crankshafts, in his Nettlestone smithy. In 1913 Arthur Creeth brought the first steam double deck bus to the island. This carried the London registration LN 4850 and was almost certainly purchased second hand from a London operator. The bus carried 34 seated passengers and was a fine addition to the fleet of single deck charabanc buses operating on the Ryde to Seaview service.

During the 1914–1918 war Creeth's buses were used to carry prisoners to building sites in various parts of the island, and to other places, to dig trenches. The firm became so busy that it

Arthur Creeth's steam-powered Darracq-Serpollet 21-seat bus, DL 502. This vehicle joined the fleet for the Seaview to Ryde service in 1910. The photograph was taken outside St. Peter's Church, Seaview.

Creeth of Nettlestone's first steam-powered double deck bus, LN 4850, is pictured at Seaview awaiting departure for Ryde. The photograph was probably taken shortly before the outbreak of the First World War in 1914. When Arthur Creeth transported this vehicle across the Solent to the Isle of Wight on a cargo boat in 1913 he was greeted by some angry Islanders. They considered such buses to be unsafe and "didn't wish to see London on the Isle of Wight."

needed to establish a semi-permanent outstation in Newport. When wartime traffic became less busy the precious buses were used for haulage work after they were converted into trucks. Some of the major jobs carried out by Creeth at this time included the laying of sewer pipes at Seaview and work for the new pumping station at the Buddle Hole, Brighstone.

In 1919 A.H. Creeth and Sons purchased a National-Clarkson (Chelmsford) steam chassis for which they constructed an open top double deck body. This vehicle, registered DL 1614, entered service in 1920. It was withdrawn by Creeth in September 1922 when it was probably the last steam bus in operation in the British Isles.

The firm continued to operate its Ryde to Seaview service throughout the 1920s trading as Premier Motor Service. During this period it used a variety of petrol engined charabanc buses and offered to take passengers on a day return excursion trip from Seaview to Portsmouth for half a crown (12.5p). This included a charabanc journey to Ryde and a trip on a Southern Railway paddle steamer across the Solent to Portsmouth Harbour station. The final steam bus, DL 1614, was converted by A.H. Creeth and Sons into a large 32-seat open coach with a Dennis petrol engine and was one of six single deck vehicles sold to Southern Vectis in 1930 when it acquired this long established independent operator.

Creeths purchased another double deck steam bus in 1919. A Clarkson-National chassis was acquired second-hand from National Steam Car Co. Ltd. and was fitted with a double deck body made by Creeths in their Nettlestone workshop. DL 1614 ran in service from 1920 to 1922 in this form. After laying disused for some time the vehicle was given an extended lease of life to 1930. Its steam engine was replaced by a Dennis petrol engine and it was fitted with a Creeth 32-seat open coach body.

10   NEWPORT (Isle of Wight). — Market Day. — LL.

St. James' Square, in the heart of Newport, was the location of the Isle of Wight's weekly livestock market for several centuries. On Tuesdays most local bus services that normally terminated in St. James' Square used nearby Quay Street. This postcard image from around 1905 shows a typical market day scene as farmers negotiated prices for cattle and sheep. The historic market was relocated to Church Litten (the site of the current Morrisons supermarket) in 1928.

3 THE DAWN OF MOTOR BUS OPERATIONS ON THE ISLAND

Contrary to popular belief there is strong evidence to suggest that the first regular Isle of Wight motor bus service was operated between Newport and Carisbrooke in 1904. A treasured original photograph in the author's collection shows an 8-seater motor wagonette, registration number DL 45, (see facing page). It is believed that this vehicle was a Daimler, manufactured in Coventry in 1903 or 1904.

This very early motor vehicle appears to have had some windows at the front and rear of the passenger saloon and a windscreen for the driver. The passenger entrance was in the middle of the back of the bus, via a high step. According to the neat sign on the roof the vehicle ran from Newport to Carisbrooke via the Simeon Monument and Cedar Hill. Unusually, fares were also displayed on this sign.

The following advertisement appeared in the Saturday 25th June 1904 issue of the Isle of Wight County Press, in the Island News, Newport and Cowes sections:-

MOTOR WAGONETTE will make hourly trips between COWES and the NEWPORT Recreation Ground for the Sports and Gala meeting. Fare 1 shilling each, either way.

Another advertisement, shown below, was placed almost every week in the same newspaper in the Island News, Newport section throughout the period Saturday 8th November 1902 to Saturday 13th May 1905:-

WARBURTON'S HOTEL BUS, first class, meets all trains and to any part of the Town or Railway, 6d – Orders received at the Hotel or by Mr A.E. Harvey, the Borough Restaurant, High Street and Mr. F.H. Bevis, Florist, St. James' Street.

Warburton's Hotel was a high quality establishment in Quay Street, until 1951 at least. The firm achieved the rare distinction for an Island business of having a royal appointment. The buildings are now part of Calvert's Hotel and there is still a sign over the ornate main entrance stating "by royal appointment to the late Queen Victoria".

It has not yet been possible to find any other 1904 notices or advertisements relating to motor wagonette or motor bus services operated by other Newport firms. It is known, however, that horse drawn stage coaches operated in the nineteenth century from Ye Olde Bugle Hotel in the High Street (now Waterstones bookshop) and the Green Dragon Inn. The latter was a very old building that was located at the junction of Town Lane and Pyle Street. It was demolished in the 1920s to enable the widening of Town Lane between Pyle Street and South Street.

From the County Press information it seems certain that a motor wagonette was being operated for a variety of local bus services and private hire work in the Newport area from June 1904 onwards, possibly starting work before that date. It is possible, but not yet proven, that this small bus was owned by Warburton's Hotel and that it was used to provide a Newport town bus service to and from the railway station until May 1905. Coincidentally, Isle of Wight Express Motor Syndicate Ltd.'s regular bus services began to operate in and around Newport in May 1905 (see next chapter). The vehicle in question was probably DL 45. It seems highly likely that it operated a regular service from Newport railway station to Carisbrooke Castle as part of its varied transport duties.

Daimler, along with Lanchester, was one of the very first manufacturers of motor cars in the UK in 1896. In February 1903 the firm took two stands at the national Motor Show, which was held at the Crystal Palace in South London. Eight different models were displayed by Daimler, including an eight-seated canopied wagonette. This demonstration vehicle was fitted with a four-cylinder motor, developing 22 b.h.p.

Vehicle registration numbers (e.g. DL 1 onwards) only became a legal requirement from January 1904 onwards. DL 45 was probably first registered on the Isle of Wight in mid 1904. The vehicle may have been new at that time or it could possibly have been manufactured slightly earlier and then issued with number plates in 1904.

NEWPORT TO SIMEON MONUMENT CEDAR HILL 1D. 2D. CARISBROOKE 3D.
DL 45

There is some additional circumstantial evidence that DL 45 was owned and operated by Warburton's Hotel. This material is contained in a 2009 Isle of Wight Family History Society member's request for information about very early DL-registered vehicles. In the request the member states that the Isle of Wight Motorists' Association was founded in November 1903 with headquarters at Warburton's Hotel. It appears that the hotel owners may have been prominent early motorists and had their own motor vehicle(s). As a matter of related interest, the inaugural motor meeting of the Association was held at Carisbrooke Castle on 27th July 1905 with a 'Motor Gymkhana'.

It is probable that Warburton's Hotel ran a high quality horse-drawn bus between the railway station and all parts of Newport up to mid-1904, by when it supplemented or replaced this vehicle with DL 45, the first motor bus on the Island. Unfortunately, following the closure of the Motor Vehicle Licensing Office at Newport, the location of the original hand written register of DL-registrations from 1903 to 1925 is unknown. This document contained precious details of the original owners and dates of initial registration of all vehicles from DL 1 to DL 4900.

There may have been a few more motor wagonettes on the Isle of Wight prior to 1905 in private ownership or possibly for commercial use, but the absence of official records makes it very difficult to provide firm evidence. The only other such vehicle known to the author is the Clement Talbot 14 h.p. wagonette DL 74, which was built in 1903. The original owner of DL 74 is unknown but it was registered to a Mr. Morris of East Cowes by 1921. It is understood that this vehicle may still exist, since a 1903 Clement Tonneau with the same registration number was contained in the national register in 2008. (ref: *Car Numbers Then and Now"* by N. Woodhall and B. Heaton).

A year after DL 45 was carrying passengers from Newport to Carisbrooke Isle of Wight Express Motor Syndicate Ltd. buses began to serve Newport with several regular services. This photograph shows one of IWEMS's double deck Milnes-Daimler vehicles in front of the former Rose and Crown public house in St. Thomas' Square in 1905.

4 ISLE OF WIGHT EXPRESS MOTOR SYNDICATE LIMITED – A TRUE PIONEER BUS OPERATOR

At the start of the Edwardian era motorbus operation in the United Kingdom was in its infancy. In his book entitled *Regional History of British Bus Services: South East England* Colin Morris states that the first regular commercial service in the South East was started in Portsmouth in January 1902 by the Portsmouth and Gosport Motor Omnibus Company Limited from the Dockyard to Fratton Park via the Town Hall. This was followed by another pioneering commercial service in Hastings and the first municipal local bus service in Eastbourne in March and April 1903 respectively. All these services were operated by single deck 16-seat Milnes-Daimler buses, based on a well engineered and reliable chassis built in Berlin by the German Daimler company. By March 1904 larger open-top 34-seat Milnes-Daimler motorbuses were in operation with the Brighton, Hove and Preston United Omnibus Company, Eastbourne Corporation and the Hastings and St. Leonards Omnibus Company.

According to David Kaye's book *Buses and Trolleybuses before 1919* there were just 31 motorbuses in use in London in 1904, compared with 3,551 horse buses. Small numbers of motor buses were also beginning to operate in other parts of the country. The Great Western Railway introduced several rural routes to feed its main line train services. The first such route, from the Lizard to Helston Station, commenced operation on 17th August 1903.

In the summer of 1904 there were probably fewer than 100 double deck motor buses operating local bus services across the whole country. Alderman A. Millward, the mayor of Ryde, was staying in Brighton for several days at this time and used the new motor buses between Brighton and Hove. Impressed by what he saw and with a keen awareness of poor local transport provision in and around his home town at that time he wished that motor buses could be introduced to the Isle of Wight. When Alderman Millward arrived home one of the first people to visit him asked if he would be willing to go into providing such a scheme on the Island. He replied that, "other things being satisfactory, I should be delighted to go into it". Within several weeks the Isle of Wight Express Motor Syndicate Ltd. was formed, with Sir Alexander Onslow as Chairman. An intensive period of company planning and development followed, including the acquisition of an office at 80 Union Street, Ryde and a large garage and workshop at Butler's Road (soon to be renamed St. John's Wood Road). The Syndicate's highly ambitious plan was to purchase seven new 36-seat double deck Milnes-Daimler motor buses and to establish a network of regular local bus services radiating from Ryde. Assisted by a dynamic operations manager the embryonic firm set about employing a team of skilled drivers, conductors and mechanics in order that a safe and reliable service could be provided for local residents and visitors. Experienced bus drivers were recruited from various parts of England, including London, Birmingham and the Great Western Railway.

Alderman Millward was determined that a high quality and progressive motor bus service would be provided for the Isle of Wight. In his speech at the luncheon at the Crown Hotel, Ryde, immediately prior to the launch of the new service on 13th April 1905, he explained that the Syndicate wished to obtain the confidence of the public. "They had done the thing quickly, but in the very best possible way, and, as the Daily Mail had reported, they were up to date. What the Island might have been years ago was a different thing from what it is today. Any community that had adopted the electric light and motor-omnibuses could not be charged with being out of date or old-fashioned. In addition to carrying passengers they had an elaborate system for carrying letters and parcels, and this was perhaps somewhat unique. At all events, wherever there was a car (bus) there would be a letter box, and in the case of their villages letters could now reach London by the time at which they were wont to be cleared. That was a distinct advantage to the people living in them. By the carriage of parcels, too, much of the inconvenience of the past would be obviated. He believed that the great benefit that the buses would bring would be to bring the people into the towns and take them from the towns to the villages, and so bring about

An early Edwardian view of two Milnes-Daimler 20 hp buses with single deck bodies. AF 66 and AF 84 were both delivered new to the Great Western Railway in 1904 and are pictured on its pioneering railway feeder service from the Lizard to Helston Station in Cornwall in that year.

a pleasant and healthy exchange between the towns and the villages."

The first four motor buses had arrived in Cowes the previous day and Alderman Millward had travelled with them in convoy to Ryde. He stated that it was a pretty sight to see them. Indulging in a kind of daydream he said it was a sort of Argosy bringing lots of good things to the shareholders and the public in general. He hoped his day dream would come true. They would have the

other cars they had ordered as soon as they could get them. They had also been disappointed as to their uniforms and letter boxes. He was sure that the fact that they had rushed the scheme through and got it in its present condition was the best assurance that the other things would come as quickly as possible. His Worship read the following telegram from a gentleman who was well known in the motor world. "Wish you all success in motor car service established today. Am sure it will be great convenience to all Islanders and render your beautiful Island more accessible to all – JOHN SCOTT MONTAGU". This was met with a strong round of applause.

Following Alderman Millward's speech Lieutenant Colonel J.F.C. Hamilton, J.P. thanked him on behalf of those present, stating that His Worship was the best Mayor in England (further applause). Councillor Hansford seconded the vote of thanks and acknowledged the Mayor's energy and attention to every detail of his duty. He had proved he was up to date by taking such an interest in that movement that they believed was the turning point in the prosperity of the Isle of Wight. (even more applause).

Shortly after the luncheon the group of VIPs travelled the short distance to Ryde Esplanade, where the official launch of the motor bus service took place, watched by huge crowds. This landmark event in the history of Isle of Wight passenger transport was recorded in a detailed report that appeared in the Isle of Wight County Press on Saturday 15th April, which is summarised in this chapter, and some historic photographs and postcards.

Lady Adela Cochrane, wife of the Deputy Governor of the Island, started the service of cars in the afternoon from the Esplanade. Here a very large crowd had assembled and the four cars were manoeuvred with the greatest ease. Lady Adela, who took up her position in the front of the leading car, said that for a very long time it had been felt to be a most important and much required thing that people should be able to move about the Island, not only with comfort but also in an inexpensive method. It was in a great measure to carry out this that the motor-cars had been brought to the Isle of Wight and the Company had been promoted. Her Ladyship read a telegram from the Commercial Motor magazine wishing the motor service every success. She was sure that those present did the same. They had no doubt realised, as she had, how very useful these cars had been in other parts of England, and hoped they would be equally so on the Island (loud applause).

Amid great cheering, Lady Adela Cochrane then started the car and the others followed it around the canoe lake and back.

THE START OF THE ISLE OF WIGHT MOTOR OMNIBUS. APRIL 13 1905.

An enormous crowd of people gathered outside the former Royal Pier Hotel at Ryde Pier Approach on 13th April 1905. They had assembled to witness the eagerly-awaited launch of the Isle of Wight Express Motor Syndicate Ltd.'s motor bus services. This photograph shows two of the brand new double deck Milnes-Daimler buses laden with VIPs and local dignatories immediately prior to the inaugural procession of the firm's initial four vehicles along Ryde Esplanade.

THE START OF THE ISLE OF WIGHT MOTOR OMNIBUSES. APRIL 13, 1905.

Milnes-Daimler bus DL 78 is captured crossing Fiveways, Ryde, observed by a gentleman cyclist. The vehicle was leaving Ryde town centre in the summer of 1905 and was probably bound for Wootton Bridge, Newport and Carisbrooke Castle.

The four cars subsequently started running to Newport, Cowes, Shanklin and Bembridge.

The Isle of Wight County Press report went on to state that the motor buses started running on their prescribed routes the following day, but owing to only four of the seven cars having been delivered the published times could not be kept. The very wet weather was unpropitious and one bus lost a (solid rubber) tyre in a muddy road just outside the Ryde Headquarters. Another operational problem occurred near Carpenters between Ryde and Brading when a bus became stuck in the mud after being driven down the wrong road. It had to be extricated with the assistance of horses and people. Faced with these teething problems and a shortage of vehicles the Board of Directors took the decision to suspend running of all services until all seven buses had reached the Island.

The map on page 32 is taken from a rare copy of the Isle of Wight Express Motor Services Ltd.'s first published timetable. It illustrates the company's ambitious plan to set up a network of regular motor bus services.

Following the well attended IWEMS launch on 13th April there was intense public interest in the new local motor bus services. Many people were keen to see the buses running regularly and to make use of them for a variety of business and social purposes. Support was not universal, however. Quite a lot of people were highly critical of the development and were quick to point out a variety of potential problems, including noise, frightening horses, damaging roads and the risk of traffic accidents. The correspondence columns in the local newspapers carried some very interesting letters – for and against – for several months.

The three delayed new buses finally arrived from the factory and the proper services commenced a few weeks later in May. Two additional Milnes-Daimler double deck buses were ordered and these joined the IWEMS fleet in July.

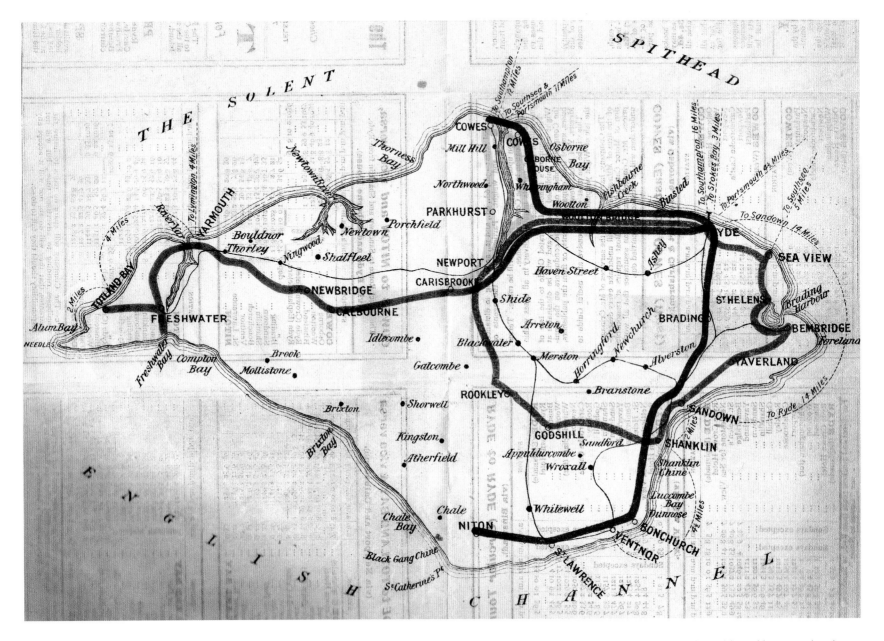

Isle of Wight Express Motor Syndicate Ltd. was a pioneer operator in many ways. From the spring of 1905 the firm issued pocket timetables with maps showing where passengers could transfer between its different services. This map included the firm's planned route from Ryde to Totland Bay which only operated for a few weeks before being withdrawn.

IWEMS Milnes-Daimler DL 78 pauses to be photographed in Victoria Avenue, Shanklin by local commercial photographer Mr Millman-Brown. The postcard picture (which would have been sold to passengers) was taken in 1905 and shows a full load of holidaymakers from Sandown and Shanklin to Carisbrooke Castle. Note the smart uniforms of the driver and conductor.

Initially the firm operated the following routes:-

- Ryde to Bembridge via Seaview and St. Helens (daily)
- Ryde to Shanklin via Brading and Sandown (daily)
- Ryde to Carisbrooke Castle via Wootton and Newport (daily)
- Ryde to West Cowes via Osborne House and East Cowes (except Tuesday and Friday)
- West Cowes to Carisbrooke Castle via Newport (except Tuesday and Friday)
- Sandown and Shanklin to Carisbrooke Castle via Godshill, Rookley and Newport (Monday, Wednesday, Thursday, Saturday and Sunday only)
- Ryde to East Cowes via Osborne House (Tuesday and Friday only)
- Sandown and Shanklin to East Cowes via Newport and Osborne House (Tuesday and Friday only)

Trips on the different routes were timed to connect as well as possible to enable passengers to undertake longer journeys if required without major delays. For example the omnibuses leaving Shanklin at 9.00am, 11.30am,

1.45pm, 4.25pm and 6.45pm connected with omnibuses leaving Ryde for Newport/Carisbrooke and Bembridge at 10.30am, 12.35pm, 3.20pm, 5.45pm and 8.15pm. Routes were chosen to be attractive to the maximum number of local residents and holidaymakers, with Carisbrooke Castle and Osborne House clearly being popular destinations for visitors in the Edwardian era. The return fare from Ryde to Bembridge was 1s. 6d. while the cost of a return journey from Sandown to Carisbrooke Castle was 2s. 6d.

During the next few months IWEMS introduced a number of route, timetable and other service alterations with details being published at frequent intervals in pocket timetables, the Isle of Wight County Press, Charpentier's, Holbrook's and other railway guides. From August 1st, the planned daily service from Ryde to Totland and Freshwater Bay via Newport, Calbourne and Yarmouth came into operation, with three journeys a day in each direction (two on a Sunday). Each complete trip from one end of the Island to the other took almost exactly three hours.

The route from Newport to the West Wight lasted only a matter of weeks before it was withdrawn, presumably mainly as a result of operational difficulties and low passenger numbers. By the beginning of September, however, two new daily services were started in the south of the Island, from Shanklin to Ventnor (journey time about 40 minutes) and from Ventnor to Blackgang (40minutes). There were three trips each way on both routes which were all timetabled to be covered by one double deck bus. Unfortunately the very hilly terrain in this part of the Island proved to be problematic for the 20 horse power vehicle and the service had to be suspended in October.

Taken overall, the pioneering network of new motor bus services proved to be very popular, especially with holidaymakers visiting the Isle of Wight. From May to October the company's buses covered over 89,000 miles and carried around 175,000 passengers. During this six month period there was just one claim made against the company, for a very minor personal injury to a passenger. Indeed IWEMS's insurers, the United Legal Indemnity Insurance Society Ltd, were so impressed with the company's excellent safety record that they allowed the company a large rebate upon the premiums agreed to be paid in consideration of the immunity from accident.

One of the biggest problems experienced in 1905 was that the nine 20 h.p. Milnes-Daimler double deck buses, although reliable, were somewhat under-powered to handle the Isle of Wight's hilly roads, particularly during poor weather. A major decision was therefore taken to replace the entire fleet (DL 75 – DL 81, DL 109 and DL 110) and these buses were sold to the London and District Motor Bus Company Ltd (fleet name Arrow) in late October 1905.

The firm placed a notice in the 7th October 1905 issue of the County Press, worded as follows:-

"NOTICE IS HEREBY GIVEN that the service of motor omnibuses between Shanklin, Ventnor and Blackgang will be suspended on and after Monday 9th October and until further notice. The directors take this opportunity of informing the inhabitants of Ventnor and the public generally that motor omnibuses especially designed to suit the roads in this district are now in course of construction.

This will enable the Company to run a greatly improved service between SHANKLIN, VENTNOR and BLACKGANG during the summer months of 1906."

During the winter of 1905/06 senior company staff worked hard to select and purchase some new motor buses that would be more suitable for Island roads and traffic conditions. There is photographic evidence that a Fiat open top double deck motor bus visited Ryde in January 1906 for an operational trial. (See image on page 36).

A strong supporter of this pioneer bus operator was Miss Cleone de Heveningham Benest (1880 – 1964). This remarkable, multi-talented Islander was born in Forest Gate, Essex and spent the first few years of her life with her mother and maternal grandparents in St Brelades in Jersey. By 1891 Cleone, mother and grandparents had moved to 11 The Strand in Ryde and ten years later the family had moved to Holly Mount, West Street, Ryde. By 1911, Cleone's grandfather had died but the three ladies were still living together "on their own means" at the same address.

Miss Benest's personal scrapbook for the period 1905 to 1911 provides a fascinating insight into this young woman's life and interests. She was a member of the Ladies' Isle of Wight Golf Club and an advanced fencer, taking part in the national finals in 1908. Her main passion, however, was for motorised transport and mechanical engineering. Miss Benest was a very early motor car driver and owner. One of her vehicles was a fine 1906 Lanchester, registration number DL 154 (see photo on page 37). She had a well equipped workshop and was adept at maintaining her own vehicles. According to a programme in her scrapbook Miss Benest participated in a competitive hill climbing trial at Lord Montagu's Beaulieu estate on 26th June 1909. In this event she recorded the fastest time of the day of 103.6 seconds in a Fiat 24/40 horse power car.

During the early 1900s Miss Benest corresponded with several motor and commercial vehicle manufacturers (including Napier and Milnes-Daimler) and visited some factories to develop her knowledge. She passed the RAC's certificates for driving and mechanical proficiency with ease and was successful in passing

For a few months in the summer of 1905 Isle of Wight Express Motor Syndicate Ltd. fitted all its double deck Milnes-Daimler buses with letter boxes. These were mounted adjacent to the passenger entrance at the rear of the vehicles, as illustrated in the photo. This innovative experiment was probably discontinued because using the boxes resulted in unacceptable delays to the scheduled bus services.

This rare photograph shows a FIAT double deck demonstration bus undergoing an operational trial with IWEMS in Ryde in January 1906. The trade plate registration number A-2-CZ indicates that the vehicle was registered in London (A) to FIAT's UK distribution premises at Long Acre (CZ).

Between 1905 and 1907 Miss Benest was given permission to drive several of the IWEMS Milnes-Daimler and Thornycroft buses. The photo to the right shows her at the wheel of Milnes-Daimler DL 81 in 1905.

the motor engineering examination held by the City and Guilds of London in 1908 when she was the only female candidate. She took every opportunity to drive motor vehicles, including lorries and buses and was allowed to drive several Isle of Wight Express Motor Syndicate Ltd. Milnes-Daimler buses in Ryde. Her scrapbook contained an original IWEMS timetable and several articles and local newspaper reports recording progress of the new local bus services.

Miss Benest also attended meetings of the Institution of Automobile Engineers, even though women were not allowed to become members at that time. A 1908 personal letter from Douglas Mackenzie, who was the final General Manager of IWEMS, was worded as follows:--

Dear Miss Benest,

Next Wednesday's meeting (of the Incorporated Institution of Automobile Engineers) has been altered to continue discussion on the subject of "front driving" and Mr. Lanchester's paper is postponed until March 11th. I enclose a ticket for next Wednesday, as if you are in Town you may like to attend.

In spite of the official ban we shall always be pleased to see you.

Yours faithfully,

Douglas Mackenzie

After a break of several months Isle of Wight Express Motor Syndicate Ltd. resumed, operating a streamlined network of local bus services from 11th April 1906. According to an article in the 31st May 1906 issue of *The Commercial Motor* the company promised to sustain its reputation as a cheap, quick and delightful method of seeing the Island. The article stated that several services were being provided, as follows:

- Circular route 1 (Ryde to Ryde via Brading, Sandown, Shanklin, Godshill, Newport, Wootton and Binstead)
- Circular route 2 (Ryde to Ryde via Binstead, Wootton, Newport, Godshill, Shanklin, Sandown and Brading)
- Bembridge to East Cowes via Seaview, Ryde, Binstead, Wootton, Whippingham and Osborne House
- Shanklin to Blackgang via Bonchurch, Ventnor, St. Lawrence and Niton

Initially the two circular routes were operated by two 36-seat open top double deck 24/40 h.p. Fiat buses (DL 131 and DL 132) while the other two routes were operated by 30 h.p. 30-seat Milnes-Daimler covered charabancs. Seven 30-seat Milnes-Daimler charabancs with bodywork constructed by the coachbuilding firm of George Mulliss and Co. of Nelson Street, Ryde were acquired between March and July (DL 129, DL 130 and DL 133 – DL 137).

The Milnes-Daimler charabancs had capacious bodies, with a closed portion at the rear. These vehicles had much more powerful engines than the 1905 double deck buses they replaced and had no difficulties with the Island's hilly roads, including the renowned Bonchurch Hill between Shanklin and Ventnor. They were able to negotiate large parts of this long, steep and twisting hill quite easily in second gear. The coachwork generally, and

Ryde was the operational base for Isle of Wight Express Motor Syndicate Ltd.'s network of local bus services. Several routes terminated at or passed through Ryde Esplanade and a well-appointed waiting room was provided at nearby 6 Pier Street (later renamed as Western Esplanade) for passengers to various Island destinations.

One of the firm's most popular services was a circular (clockwise and anti-clockwise) route from Ryde to Ryde via Brading, Sandown, Shanklin, Godshill and Newport. This photograph shows one of the 30 h.p. single deck Milnes-Daimler buses that operated on the route in 1906.

the roll-up blinds in particular, added distinctly to the comfort of the passengers both in wet and sunny weather. In contrast to the original buses that operated the previous year there are very few known photographs/ postcards of the more powerful Milnes-Daimler single deck charabancs, Fiat double deck buses and Thornycroft charabancs that served the Island in 1906 and 1907. This is probably because the initial double deck buses had much greater novelty value.

All buses leaving Ryde or Newport for Shanklin were timed to connect at Shanklin with the Ventnor and Blackgang service and vice versa. Special five shilling (25p) day tickets, available over all the company's routes, were issued. These enabled passengers to traverse much of the Island in one day and to break their journeys at discretion. This was an early, albeit very expensive, version of a rover ticket or travelcard. More than fifty years later London Transport Green and Red Rover tickets for children under sixteen cost exactly the same! Another innovative aspect of the company's work was express parcel delivery. Parcels not exceeding 20 pounds in weight were carried on the motor buses and delivered within one mile of the various agents' offices, at small inclusive charges. For added convenience parcels could alternatively be handed to bus conductors en route.

In Pier Street, Ryde, very close to the bus services' starting point at the Esplanade, the company provided a comfortable and well-appointed waiting room and reading room for prospective passengers. It was furnished with cosy basket chairs and copies of various pictorial magazines and newspapers were always available. There was also an enquiry office where relevant information on all bus services could be obtained. The picture on page 38 shows this splendid 'departure lounge' facility.

In early May a revised timetable was introduced. The main changes were:

- The introduction of a high frequency service from East Cowes (Pontoon and Floating Bridge) to Osborne House with departures every 10 minutes.
- A new outer circular route from Ryde to Ryde via Seaview, St. Helens, Bembridge, Sandown, Shanklin, Godshill, Newport and Wootton (one journey in each direction on Monday, Wednesday, Thursday, Saturday and Sunday).
- Slightly increased number of journeys on the main Ryde to Ryde circular tours, the Bembridge to East Cowes via Ryde and Osborne House service and the Shanklin to Blackgang via Ventnor route.

Further changes followed at the beginning of July:

- The withdrawal of the high frequency service from East Cowes to Osborne House.
- The withdrawal of the outer circular route from Ryde to Ryde via Bembridge.
- The introduction of a new route from East Cowes to West Cowes via Osborne, Newport, Carisbrooke, Newport, Parkhurst and Northwood.
- A new once-daily round the Island tour commencing from Ryde at 10.45am and returning to Ryde at 5.47pm. Route via Brading, Sandown, Shanklin, Ventnor, Blackgang (for lunch), Chale, Shorwell, Brighstone, Brook, Freshwater (for tea), Chessell, Calbourne, Carisbrooke, Newport, Wootton and Binstead. This service was timed to connect with ferries from and to Southsea.

- A new twice a week (Tuesday and Friday) service from Ryde, Sandown and Shanklin to Osborne House via Carisbrooke and Newport. Buses departed from Ryde at 10.15am and arrived at Osborne House at 12.45pm. Passengers had 4.5 hours to look at Osborne House before the return bus departed at 5pm, arriving back at Ryde at 7.21pm via Newport, Shanklin and Sandown.

In the 4th August issue of the County Press, a few weeks after the tragic Handcross Hill bus accident north of Brighton, Isle of Wight Express Motor Syndicate Ltd. printed an IMPORTANT NOTICE, worded virtually as follows:

"The Directors beg to announce that on and after 6th August a half-hourly service will be run during Cowes Week between West Cowes and Carisbrooke Castle, and the Shanklin to Blackgang route will be resumed. As from that date, the full service (other than East Cowes to West Cowes), as published in the Company's timetables, will be run. After the date mentioned additional omnibuses will be available in the Island, which will be available for spare omnibuses. The Directors believe that with the aid of these spare omnibuses the whole of the service will be maintained without intermission. On and after 6th August, the Full Service of motor charabancs will be resumed throughout the Island, according to the Company's timetable. Timetables and map of the Island (showing all routes in five different colours), are available gratis at the Company's office and from all Agents. On and after 13th August the Cowes East to Cowes West route will be resumed.

GREAT REDUCTION IN FARES OFFERED FOR GROUPS OF PEOPLE BUYING DAY TICKETS AND THOSE TRAVELLING ON ROUND THE ISLAND TOURS

Each charabanc bears a certificate, signed by the Company's Works Manager every day, as to the efficiency of the brakes."

Special notices regarding fare reductions and vehicle safety were printed weekly in the County Press during August. Then at the end of August a supplementary service was introduced between Ryde and Seaview (5 return journeys per day) to cope with the large increase in traffic experienced in this part of the Island. In addition the firm started to operate two new return journeys per day between Seaview and Shanklin.

Towards the end of the summer season another revised timetable was published that came into effect from 1st October 1906 until further notice. There were just three services – Ryde to Newport, Ryde to Sandown and Shanklin and Ryde to Seaview and St. Helens. On the Ryde to Newport service there were six return journeys daily (three on Sundays). From Ryde to Sandown and Shanklin there were four return journeys daily (two on Sundays) while there were seven return journeys daily between Ryde and Seaview (three on Sundays). The timetable also included details of reduced fares (e.g. Ryde to Seaview 6d, Ryde to Brading 6d, Ryde to Sandown 8d, Ryde to Shanklin 9d, Ryde to Wootton Bridge 5d, Ryde to Newport 9d, Sandown to Shanklin 3d). An original copy of this timetable is displayed in the Isle of Wight Bus and Coach Museum.

The third and final year of Isle of Wight Express Motor Syndicate Ltd's bus operation commenced on 27th March 1907. By this time Douglas Mackenzie, a London-based consulting engineer for mechanical transport had been appointed as General Manager in a bid to turn around the company's fortunes. Reduced fares for all routes were publicised in an effort to increase the number of passengers. The first published timetable for 1907 showed that the firm had chosen to focus on the following three routes:-

- Ryde to Newport and Carisbrooke Castle (five return journeys per weekday, less on Sundays)
- Ryde to Sandown and Shanklin (seven return journeys per weekday, less on Sundays)
- Ryde to Seaview and St. Helens (six return journeys per weekday, less on Sundays)

From 6th April the number of return journeys on the Ryde to Sandown and Shanklin service was reduced from seven to four. Then, in a final roll of the dice Mackenzie published a further revised timetable on the front page of the County Press on Saturday 18th May, as follows:-

---

ISLE OF WIGHT MOTOR OMNIBUSES
Services and Fares
From May 17th to July 27th, 1907
(unless previously withdrawn)

Ryde, Seaview, St. Helens and Bembridge (8 return journeys)
Ryde, Newport and Carisbrooke Castle (6 return journeys)
Ryde, Sandown and Shanklin (4 return journeys)
West Cowes, Newport and Carisbrooke Castle (7 return journeys)
Ryde Suburban Service (not Sundays) (4 return journeys)

In addition a number of special Sunday excursion trips were advertised:

11.15am Ryde, Ashey Down, Newchurch, Shanklin, Sandown, Brading, Ryde
12.30pm Golfers' special. Shanklin, Sandown and St. Helens
2.10pm Ryde, Ashey Down, Arreton Down, Newport

Return fares of 2s 6d
Passengers permitted to return to Ryde by any afternoon omnibus

---

Isle of Wight Express Motor Syndicate Ltd. continued to struggle on through the summer of 1907 with a combination of local bus services and private hire work. A couple of further revised timetables were introduced and the final "winter" timetable came into effect from 30th September. This included just three services, Ryde to St. Helens via Seaview, Ryde to West Cowes via Newport and Ryde to Shanklin via Sandown. It has not been possible to determine exactly when services ceased but this probably occurred towards the end of October. Thus this bold and innovative pioneer bus operator which carried the hopes of many people on the Island moved inexorably towards liquidation. Douglas Mackenzie, who otherwise had a glittering career in the bus industry, was handed the task of acting as official receiver. He arranged for the company's assets, including the remaining buses, to be sold by early 1908.

The firm should be credited with several achievements during its three year life. These include:-

- Very successful launch event in April 1905
- High level of local support to improve accessibility from villages to towns
- The creation of a network of bus routes
- The operation of at least 22 buses, including 11 double deck vehicles, between 1905 and 1907
- The introduction of an early "travelcard" ticket, permitting travel on the whole network
- The short-lived parcel and letter services
- The production of pocket timetables and route maps for passengers
- The provision of a comfortable central waiting room at Ryde, the hub of the network
- An excellent driver safety record

Perhaps the key internal and external reasons for the firm's demise were:-

- Delay to the start of the service in 1905 caused by late delivery of three buses
- Over-ambitious plans to develop a major network of routes too soon
- Technical difficulties (e.g. the 20h.p. 1905 buses were underpowered for the Island's hilly roads)
- Local opposition from various sectors, especially those involved in horse-drawn transport
- The tragic Handcross bus accident in July 1906 that jolted the public's confidence in this form of travel
- IWEMS introduced far too many route and timetable alterations
- Fares were too expensive for local residents
- Huge expense of having to buy a new fleet of vehicles after the first six months of operation
- The seasonal nature of the visitor aspect of the business
- Competition from the railways and horse-drawn coaches
- Summer-only service caused staff and passenger retention problems
- Burden of inflated expectations for the success of the new bus services
- Major disputes between Directors in 1906, as recorded in detailed correspondence in the County Press

5 TRANSITION FROM HORSE-DRAWN TO MOTOR BUSES AND CHARABANCS

The change from horse-drawn to motorised bus services on the Isle of Wight was gradual. Right up to the early 1920s the two modes of road passenger transport operated side by side, sometimes in direct competition. Following the bold but ultimately unsuccessful business venture of Isle of Wight Express Motor Syndicate Ltd. few other operators were prepared to set up new local bus services with petrol-engined or steam-powered vehicles. The situation was not helped by public awareness of a serious traffic accident that happened at Handcross in Sussex and widespread concern about the safety of this new mechanical type of public transport. On 12th July 1906 a London Motor Omnibus Company Ltd. (Vanguard) double deck Milnes-Daimler bus travelling from Orpington to Brighton had run out of control and left the road on Handcross Hill with the tragic loss of ten lives.

These were still very early days in the development of the motor bus and there were few reliable and affordable vehicles being produced, especially by UK manufacturers. The Daimler Company of Germany managed to secure a large part of the UK

Graphic evidence of the serious traffic accident that occurred at Handcross Hill in July 1906. Tragically ten people lost their lives when the driver lost control of this double deck Milnes-Daimler bus.

market up to around 1910 with its rather noisy but well engineered bus chassis, which were normally bodied in England. Restrictive regulations meant that buses could not carry more than 36 seated passengers (18 upstairs and 18 downstairs) and speeds in excess of 12 miles per hour were not permitted.

In London, motor buses first outnumbered horse buses in 1910, when there were 1,200 motorised and 1,103 horse-drawn vehicles. It was probably a full ten years later, however, when this situation occurred on the Isle of Wight.

The onset of the First World War meant that bus operators were no longer permitted to import German vehicles. From 1913 onwards virtually all the country's vehicle manufacturing resources were channelled towards producing military vehicles and many existing buses and commercial vehicles were requisitioned by the armed forces to serve at home or in mainland Europe.

Apart from the ten or so steam-powered buses acquired by A.H. Creeth and Sons (Premier Motor Service) of Nettlestone very few DL-registered or mainland-registered motor buses were purchased for use on the Island up to 1921. An exception was the local service operated in and around Ventnor by Ventnor Road Cars Ltd. between 1913 and 1914. This firm was developed by a consortium of local businessmen. A rare photo of a Ventnor Road Cars Ltd. single deck Commer bus (probably registered LF 9966) is shown on the next page. This picture was taken close to The Volunteer Public House in Victoria Street, Ventnor, just before the First World War. The Volunteer was then the main meeting place for local bus and charabanc drivers between duties.

The informative unpublished document *Isle of Wight Registrations in the Original DL-Series* by Don Vincent and Chris Roberts records 66 new buses and charabancs between DL 1 and DL 2000 registered up to 1921. It is interesting to note that only 45 of these vehicles were delivered to Isle of Wight operators. Many of the registration numbers were reserved by Douglas Mackenzie in 1906/1907 for future buses for Isle of Wight Express Motor Syndicate Ltd. before this firm went into liquidation. After IWEMS ceased trading he continued to have an office in Ryde and to reserve Isle of Wight DL registrations for new buses and charabancs for other bus operators he was involved with. Mackenzie went on to have an illustrious career in the bus industry, notably with the prestigious Southdown Motor Services Ltd. in Sussex. The picture on page 46 shows a bearded Douglas Mackenzie standing alongside a Daimler CC-type coach, registration number DL 705. This 'slipper-bodied' vehicle was photographed in Keswick during a very early long-distance tour of the Lake District that Mackenzie organised for Worthing Motor Services Ltd. (fleetname Sussex Tourist Coaches) in 1914.

Several firms continued to provide regular horse-drawn buses and coaches right up to the 1920s. Such vehicles were particularly popular with visitors to the Island and were part of many people's holiday experience for trips to places like Osborne House and Blackgang Chine. Vanner's of Ryde was one of the last firms to operate horse-drawn stage coaches and it began operating a motor bus service in 1929. As Hayles and Vanner (Supreme Bus Service) the firm ran a frequent daily service from Ryde to Newport via Haylands and Havenstreet. This service continued until 1933 when the route licence and two 20-seat buses, a General Motors T30 and a Bedford WLG, both with stylish Grose Ltd. bodywork, were sold to Southern Vectis. The publicity cards on page 49 provide an interesting glimpse of Vanner's horse-drawn services in the early twentieth century.

Horse-drawn coaches provided regular railway and ferry feeder services until after the First World War in areas like Ventnor and the West Wight, while horse-drawn coach and carriage excursions from Ryde, Cowes and Yarmouth were popular in the summer months. In addition many major hotels carried on providing horse-drawn transport for their customers, both to and from the nearest railway station and also for day and half day excursions to places of interest. From around 1920 onwards, however, these forms of transport declined fairly rapidly as motor buses and charabancs became more popular.

The list on page 50 gives brief details of all known DL-registered motor buses and charabancs between DL 1 and DL 2000 that were delivered up to 1921. For more information on these and other Isle of Wight public service vehicles up to 1935 readers are recommended to refer to Don Vincent and Chris Roberts' excellent document on DL-registered vehicles, a copy of which is held at the Isle of Wight Record Office.

In Ventnor, the southernmost town on the Isle of Wight, a local town bus service was introduced by Ventnor Road Cars Ltd. in 1913. One of the firm's vehicles linking the shops, hotels and residential areas with the two railway stations was this fine rear entrance single deck Commer bus. The short-lived service was withdrawn in 1914.

Following the demise of Isle of Wight Express Motor Syndicate Ltd. Douglas Mackenzie had a glittering career in the bus industry. One of his many successful innovations was the development of long distance motor coach tours. The bearded Mackenzie is seen standing beside the driver's cab in this photograph of Isle of Wight registered Daimler 30-seat coach DL 705. The vehicle was at Keswick Hotel in 1914 on a Sussex Tourist Coaches tour to the Lake District.

This superb pre-First World War photograph of Ryde Esplanade contains a wide range of horse-drawn and motor vehicles. In the middle of the picture are a pair of Creeth steam-powered single deck buses on the Ryde to Seaview local bus service.

In 1907 Douglas Mackenzie leased eight 24 h.p. 30-seat Thornycroft charabancs, registered as DL 203 – DL 210, for IWEMS. Only four of these (DL 203 – DL 206) are believed to have worked on the Island. The other four, including DL 209 with "slipper" tiered-seating bodywork, were used in Clacton-on-Sea or Worthing.

Several more DL-registered buses were operated by Mackenzie for Worthing Motor Services Ltd. (a predecessor of Southdown Motor Services Ltd.). This photograph shows DL 621, a double deck Straker-Squire vehicle on the firm's Worthing to Tarring service, around 1914.

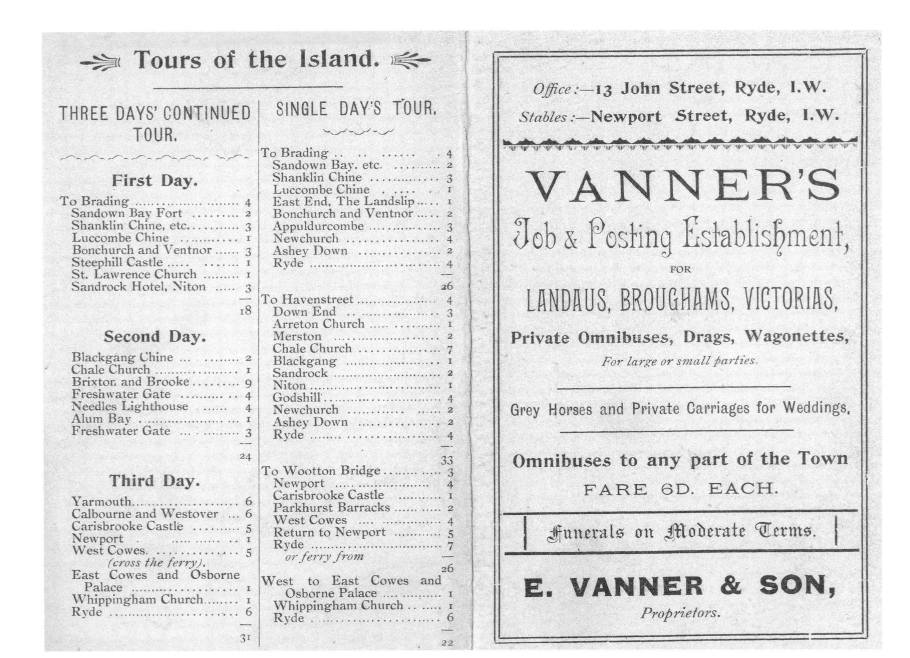

Tours of the Island.

THREE DAYS' CONTINUED TOUR.

First Day.

To Brading	4
Sandown Bay Fort	2
Shanklin Chine, etc.	3
Luccombe Chine	1
Bonchurch and Ventnor	3
Steephill Castle	1
St. Lawrence Church	1
Sandrock Hotel, Niton	3
	18

Second Day.

Blackgang Chine	2
Chale Church	1
Brixton and Brooke	9
Freshwater Gate	4
Needles Lighthouse	4
Alum Bay	1
Freshwater Gate	3
	24

Third Day.

Yarmouth	6
Calbourne and Westover	6
Carisbrooke Castle	5
Newport	1
West Cowes	5
(cross the ferry).	
East Cowes and Osborne Palace	1
Whippingham Church	1
Ryde	6
	31

SINGLE DAY'S TOUR.

To Brading	4
Sandown Bay. etc.	2
Shanklin Chine	3
Luccombe Chine	1
East End, The Landslip	1
Bonchurch and Ventnor	2
Appuldurcombe	3
Newchurch	4
Ashey Down	2
Ryde	4
	26
To Havenstreet	4
Down End	3
Arreton Church	1
Merston	2
Chale Church	7
Blackgang	1
Sandrock	2
Niton	1
Godshill	4
Newchurch	2
Ashey Down	2
Ryde	4
	33
To Wootton Bridge	3
Newport	4
Carisbrooke Castle	1
Parkhurst Barracks	2
West Cowes	4
Return to Newport	5
Ryde	7
or ferry from	
	26
West to East Cowes and Osborne Palace	1
Whippingham Church	1
Ryde	6
	22

Vanner's of Ryde produced an interesting publicity leaflet for their horse-drawn coach tours on the Isle of Wight. This version of the document is believed to date from around 1910.

DL-registered buses and charabancs (1904 – 1921)

- DL 45 (8-seat Daimler motor wagonette, used on Newport – Carisbrooke Castle service in 1904)
- DL 75 – DL 81, DL 109/110 (9 IWEMS Milnes-Daimler 36-seat 20hp open top double deck buses), 1905
- DL 129/130, DL 133 – DL 137 (7 IWEMS Milnes-Daimler 28/30hp 30-seat single deck buses), 1906
- DL 131/132 (Two IWEMS FIAT 24/40hp open top double deck buses), 1906
- DL 192 Thornycroft 28h.p. charabanc. 1907(?)
- DL 203 – 210 inclusive (8 Thornycrofts – 7 charabancs and 1 bus) (DL 203-206 used by IWEMS), 1907
- DL 254 – 256 (3 Milnes Daimler vehicles, 1 charabanc and 2 double deck buses) that ran in Torquay, 1907
- DL 261 (MOC coach) that operated in Sussex, 1908
- DL 299 – Gardner-Serpollet steam powered charabanc with Creeth body, A.H. Creeth and Sons, 1908
- DL 371 (Milnes-Daimler charabanc) that operated in Sussex, 1908
- DL 381 – 384 or 385 (Milnes-Daimler charabancs) that operated in Sussex, 1908
- DL 493 (Leyland X4 bus), operated by Worthing Motor Services Ltd. from 1913, then to Southdown, 1915
- DL 502 Darracq-Serpollet steam bus, A.H. Creeth and Sons, 1910
- DL 621 (Straker Squire bus) that operated in Sussex, 1912
- DL 701 – 706 (Daimler coaches) that operated in Sussex, 1913/1914
- DL 753 De Dietrich 14-seat charabanc, new to Coombes Brothers, Shanklin, 1913
- DL 780 Napier 23-seat charabanc, owned by Mrs. Mary Bartlett, Shanklin, 1913 (named Yellow Peril)
- DL 983 Ford wagonette, owned by A. Cooper, Freshwater by 1921
- DL 1047 Dennis 14-seat charabanc, new to G. Luscombe, Shanklin, date unknown, then Coombes Bros.
- DL 1073 Overland 65 charabanc with 26 seats, R.C. Cooper, Brighstone by 26.1.1921
- DL 1274 Garford 14-seat charabanc, J. Gillan, Freshwater, date unknown

- DL 1461 Leyland 36-seat charabanc, Fountain Garage Ltd., Cowes in June 1919
- DL 1463 Dennis charabanc with Creeth 26-seat body in June 1919, A.H. Creeth and Sons
- DL 1536 Unic 14-seat charabanc, Coombes Brothers, Shanklin by 1921
- DL 1614 National-Clarkson steam chassis with Creeth double deck body, probably 1919
- DL 1671 Napier 15-seat charabanc, Taylor's Garage, Ryde, 1920, later to A.H. Creeth and Sons
- DL 1779 Dennis charabanc with Creeth 26-seat body, A.H. Creeth and Sons
- DL 1807 Lancia RTC charabanc with 14-seat body, S.W.M. Blundell, Shanklin by May 1921
- DL 1808 Whiting 20-seat charabanc, A. Cooper, Freshwater by 1921
- DL 1824 Leyland charabanc, Sandown Motor Touring Company Ltd., in 1920
- DL 1827 Daimler W with 29-seat body by F. Sivell, Ventnor, E.H. Crinage, Ventnor by March 1921
- DL 1875 Daimler CB charabanc with 24-seat body, Coombes Brothers, Shanklin, 1920
- DL 1888 Ford 18-seat bus, with ex-Read's horse-drawn bus body, F.A. Colson, Carisbrooke by 1921
- DL 1911 Leyland 24-seat charabanc, W.R. Taylor, Ryde by February 1921
- DL 1932 Ford 13-seat bus, A.T. Barton, Newport by February 1921
- DL 1935 Garford 19-seat charabanc, H.P. Coleman, Sandown by February 1921
- DL 1997 Leyland charabanc with 28-seat body, A. Cooper, Freshwater, 1921

There were also a number of non-DL registered buses and charabancs that entered service with Isle of Wight independent operators during this period but it is generally more difficult to trace their official records and details. There is photographic evidence of several such vehicles (e.g. OS 41 and LN 4850 of A.H. Creeth and Sons (Premier Motor Service), LF 9966 of Ventnor Road Cars Ltd and BN 1954 of Sandown Touring Company).

6 RAPID GROWTH OF INDEPENDENT OPERATORS IN THE 1920s

In the years immediately after the First World War economic, social and political conditions were all favourable for a major expansion of local motor bus services in the Isle of Wight that had been delayed for over a decade. Many buses which had been requisitioned for the war effort at home and in mainland Europe became available for civilian duties once more. A good example was the solid-tyred, 29-seat Belsize charabanc "Sandown Queen", registration BN 1954, shown below, operated by J.H. Thomas

and F.C. Fanner (Sandown Touring Co.) on a private hire outing in September 1919. Note the interesting position of the driver, Charlie Fanner, flanked by passengers on both sides, the extremely open nature of the vehicle and the antiquated headlamps. This photo was taken at the rear of the Sandringham Hotel, Lower High Street, Sandown.

Buses and charabancs began to roll off the factory production lines again for domestic use and a number of firms looked to set up new local transport services for both residents and holidaymakers. Some of these firms were supported by investors from the mainland (e.g. Dodson and Campbell Ltd.), others were established Isle of Wight firms who sought to diversify into this area of work (e.g. the carrier G.A. Shotter of Brighstone) and a third group of firms were brand new. A number of these new firms were started by ex-servicemen who had returned from the war and were keen to make good use of their recently acquired bus driving and maintenance skills (e.g. Alexander Harvey Hunter's Pioneer Bus Service of Ryde).

After a number of years of severe austerity and in a period of low car ownership there were profits to be made by firms which could provide quick, reliable and affordable bus services, especially during the busy summer months. In the lightly-regulated environment of the 1920s it was fairly easy for operators to start running local services and competition for passengers was intense, especially on the busiest corridors such as Cowes to Newport, Newport to Ryde, Newport to Sandown and Newport to Carisbrooke. It was not uncommon to have two or three firms involved in fierce on-the-road commercial battles and operators often employed and accused each other of using a variety tactics to cream off the traffic on lucrative routes, some of them being commercially aggressive or even underhand. Such tactics included running vehicles just in front of their rival's buses in an attempt to be first to pick up passengers along the route. As the decade progressed new firms seeking to enter the market were typically viewed unfavourably by the larger, more established operators, and they had to be extremely resourceful, determined and thick-skinned to develop and retain a regular and loyal clientele.

In order to attract the maximum number of passengers in this fiercely competitive environment operators adopted a number of approaches to make their services as attractive and distinctive as possible. These included smart fleet liveries, clear destination boards/ blinds, low fares, friendly customer care, reliable, comfortable and attractive vehicles, frequent journeys and punctuality.

Colson Brothers of Carisbrooke, for example, faced very strong competition from Vectis Bus Company, Arthur Thomas Barton, Albert Edward King, Brown's Bus Service and G.A. Shotter and Sons on the short, busy and lucrative route from Newport to Carisbrooke during the 1920s. From the date when the firm commenced operation in 1920 Colson Brothers sought to provide a highly personalised customer service, sometimes dropping regular customers and their shopping at their front doors. As a special feature to reinforce brand identity and customer loyalty the firm employed a characteristic small green light above the driver's cab of its buses. It also displayed very clear destination boards. In the mid-1920s St. James' Square was becoming very congested, partly because so many bus operators were using it as their Newport terminus. Colsons were required by Newport Council to set down and pick up passengers in nearby Lugley Street but the firm argued successfully that it was unfair that they should not be allowed to use St. James' Square side by side with Vectis Bus Company and their other competitors.

The photo opposite, which was a popular Newport postcard, shows a typical view of St. James' Square in the mid-1920s. This illustrates the large number of small buses that terminated in the square and the lines of vehicles that formed prior to departing to many parts of the Island. The bus in the centre of the picture, DL 1932, was a 13-seat Ford which was operated on local services by A.T. Barton in the early 1920s.

On the Cowes to Newport corridor major competition occurred at this time between three of the largest bus operators – Fowler's Royal Blue, Vectis Bus Company and Enterprise Bus Service with a fourth firm (Annie Bennett's Red Bus Service of Northwood) providing another parallel service for a short time from 1925 to 1926.

MARKET PLACE, NEWPORT. I. O. W

Fowler's Royal Blue 26-seat Daimler bus, DL 2713, in Albert Street, Ventnor, around 1922. Note the solid tyres and illuminated Royal Blue sign above the driver's cab.

Fowler's Royal Blue ran a number of high quality Daimler buses from Cowes to Newport and from Newport to Ventnor from 1921, but ceased operating local services to concentrate on coach excursions and private hire work around 1927.

There was quite a high turnover of independent operators and the situation changed from one year to the next with regard to the number of operators and the services they provided. Some found the daily rigours of local bus service operation and competition too much and were happy to be bought out by a larger rival or turned to other business activities, such as the operation of coach excursions and private hire work. Others, such as Wavell's Enterprise Bus Service, G.A. Shotter and Sons and Newell's Express Motor Service, managed to do quite well and succeeded in running efficient and well-patronised stage carriage services on

Colsons' 20-seat Dennis bus DL 6210 waits in St. James' Square, Newport for passengers to Carisbrooke. New in 1929 this sturdy vehicle shows the distinctive green light above the letter 'S' on the Colsons' sign that was a special feature of all the firm's buses at that time.

the Island for over 30 years. Most of the independent operators employed fairly small 14-seater and 20-seater buses in this period, especially on the rural routes. These vehicles were built by a wide variety of manufacturers. Daimler, Dennis, Ford, Guy and Chevrolet buses were popular but many other types were also present, such as Morris, Commer and Graham Brothers. A few operators (e.g. Brown's Bus Service, Walkden's and Wavell's Enterprise Bus Service) also purchased some larger single deck buses for use on the busier longer routes (e.g. Leyland and Dennis vehicles) while Enterprise and Creeths operated a small number of open top double deck vehicles for a few years. A 1920s' Enterprise double deck bus is shown in the photo on the following page, on the Newport to Sandown service.

Wavell's Enterprise Bus Service operated this open top solid-tyred double deck bus on its Newport to Sandown local service in the late 1920s.

7 A SNAPSHOT IN TIME – THE ISLAND'S LOCAL BUS SERVICES IN 1928

The number of independent bus operators on the Isle of Wight reached its peak in the late 1920s. Several firms including Fowler's Royal Blue and A.T. Barton had ceased running local bus services after a few years but it is believed that there were at least 23 separate businesses running regular stage carriage bus services in 1928. These provided an extensive network of road passenger transport services across the Island and there were several examples of direct on-the-road competition taking place between two or three operators on the busiest and most lucrative routes. In addition there were still many long-established carriers conveying people from outlying villages to Newport and Ryde. Some of these enterprising businesses provided seats for small numbers of passengers in the motorised lorries they purchased in the early 1920s to replace their outmoded horse-drawn vans. The last horse-drawn carrier's van on the Island was owned by Edwin Holbrook who operated his regular goods and passengers service from Newtown and Porchfield to Newport from 1902 until his retirement in 1925.

Much of the following information in this chapter has been drawn from an article written by F.H.W. Green, entitled *Isle of Wight Services – Thirty Years On*. It appeared in the November 1958 issue of *Buses Illustrated* and provides an informed account of the routes and vehicles operated in 1928, the year before Southern Vectis Omnibus Company Ltd. was formed.

The largest operator was Dodson Brothers Ltd. (Vectis Bus Company) which had commenced bus operation in 1921. By 1928 this firm had over 30 single deck buses, chiefly on Daimler, Guy and ADC chassis. Ten 32-seater ADCs fitted with Daimler 6 cylinder petrol engines and two 14-seater Chevrolets were the most recent additions to the fleet, which was based at depots in Newport and Somerton. The Vectis routes were:

- Ryde to Cowes via Sandown, Shanklin, Godshill and Newport
- Gurnard to Ryde via Cowes, Parkhurst, Newport and Wootton
- Ventnor to Shanklin via Bonchurch

- Newport to East Cowes via Whippingham and Osborne
- Newport to Freshwater/Alum Bay via Carisbrooke, Shorwell and Brook
- Newport to Ventnor via Chale and Niton
- Newport to Ventnor via Godshill, Whitwell and Niton
- Newport to Cowes via Marks Corner and Gurnard
- Newport to Carisbrooke

There were frequent services between Newport and nearby Carisbrooke by Vectis, Colson Brothers and A.E. King's buses, with extensions to Gunville by the two latter firms. King's buses also ran daily to Parkhurst and Camp Hill and a return journey was made to the former County Psychiatric Hospital at Whitecroft every Monday.

The second largest fleet was operated by Wavell's Enterprise Bus Service, which also started business in 1921. Ten buses were garaged in the firm's centrally located premises in South Street, Newport. There were five Morrises and two Fords (all 14-seaters), two Daimler 20-seaters and one AEC 24-seater. Enterprise's routes were:

- Newport to Cowes via Marks Corner
- Newport to East Cowes via Whippingham
- Newport to Sandown via Arreton and Apse Heath
- East Cowes to Ryde via Wootton and Binstead

F. & S.P. Boxall of Godshill ran a regular service from Newport to Sandown via Godshill and Shanklin with several Fords and a Graham Brothers' bus in competition with Vectis and Walkden's Bus Service of Sandown on this route. Yet another operator, Cyril Cooke of Newchurch, ran a service from Newport to Sandown, his route running via Newchurch and Lake. Walkden's buses also operated a service between Shanklin and Ryde and inter-available tickets were issued with Boxalls, at least between Sandown and Shanklin. Walkden's employed three Morris buses on the Shanklin to Ryde service and another between Sandown, Whitecliffe Bay and Bembridge, a route which was also covered by L.J. Dallimore of Bembridge and by F.D. Lawson's Regel Bus Service of Shanklin. The latter operated the most frequent service on this route, using a smart 14-seater Dennis with a Short Brothers' body. Lawson's Regel Bus Service also had a route between Shanklin and Ventnor via Wroxall.

Several short distance bus services ran from Ryde and three operators concerned were unique in the Isle of Wight at that time in running open charabancs, with weather hoods, on stage carriage services. They were Frank Plater's Isle of Wight Tourist Company of Ryde which ran to St. Helen's, A.H. Creeth and Sons of Nettlestone (Premier Motor Service) which ran its long-established route to Seaview, and Newell's Express Motor Service (to become Seaview Services Ltd) which also ran to Seaview. The following photograph taken around that time shows two competing Newell's and Creeth's charabancs waiting at Ryde Pier Approach to take passengers to Seaview.

Pioneer Bus Service ran local routes from Ryde to Haylands and Elmfield. This company was owned by Alexander Harvey Hunter of Wootton. Mr Hunter served his country in India during the First World War. Following his return to the Isle of Wight in

No. 9   Pier Approach, Ryde

1919 he trained as a motor engineer before founding Pioneer Bus Service in 1924. He operated these local bus services from 1924 to 1931 before selling the firm to his brother-in-law Charles Alfred Coffen. Mr Coffen continued to run the popular Pioneer Bus Service until 1937 when the company was acquired by Southern Vectis, including its mixed fleet of six small buses. The following photo shows an attractive pair of Pioneer Chevrolet 14-seaters DL 4854 and DL 5211 outside the Colonnade, Ryde.

In addition to the Vectis service on the major route between Ryde and Newport there were also F.W. Casey of Ryde, which operated via Wootton and Barton Henry Bullock's Surprise Bus Service of Havenstreet, which ran via Havenstreet. Casey's 20-seat Guy buses were renowned for their excellent turn of speed on the Ryde to Newport road and frequently outperformed the heavy Daimlers of their Vectis rivals. One of these so-called "chaser" vehicles, DL 5277, is shown on the following page in Southern Vectis livery at Somerton. It was one of three such vehicles owned by Casey that were acquired by Southern Vectis when it

bought out the fledgling rival firm in 1929. The bus was new in 1927 and it continued to operate on Island roads until 1935.

In the West Wight most routes focused on Freshwater and the Vectis services were less in evidence than elsewhere. Pink Brothers and Coopers ran local services in Freshwater, Totland Bay and Yarmouth, in connection with trains and with the Yarmouth to Lymington ferry. Brown's Bus Service of Carisbrooke and Totland ran between Freshwater and district and Newport by several routes, all of which passed through Carisbrooke and Ningwood. They operated several different makes of buses including Dennis and Morris. In addition Hilton Herbert Hall's West Wight Bus Service operated two Graham Brothers' buses and a Dodge 20-seater DL 5709 (see page 93) on the main road between Newport, Shalfleet, Yarmouth and Freshwater.

According to Derek Sprake in his book *Put out the flag* there was extremely fierce on-the-road competition on this corridor from Newport to the West Wight between Hilton Hall's West Wight Bus Service and Brown's Bus Service. This competition eventually forced Hall to sell his business to Brown's Bus Service in 1931, following many arguments and incidents.

Finally in the southern part of the Isle of Wight G.A. Shotter and Sons ran a service from Brook to Newport via Brighstone and Shorwell. Unusually, this service terminated in St. Thomas's Square rather than the main bus station in St. James's Square, reflecting the fact that Shotter's horse-drawn carrier's service had used the former King's Head in Pyle Street and St. Thomas's Square as its Newport base for over 100 years. Andrew Leslie Morris of Niton operated a rural service from Chale to Ventnor via Niton and Whitwell, J.E.R. Daish (White Star) ran a service from Chale/ Blackgang to Newport via Chillerton and Millicent Brown (Brown's Bus) operated a Ventnor town service.

This photo shows a pair of Coopers' buses (REO AG 6491 and Studebaker DL 7596) in Yarmouth. These buses worked mainly in the West Wight, and the picture was probably taken around 1931.

8 HARRY MARGHAM AND SONS LTD. – A MAJOR COACHBUILDER IN NEWPORT

The most important coachbuilding and vehicle body repair business in the Isle of Wight in the twentieth century was undoubtedly Harry Margham and Sons Ltd. of Newport. The founder of this family firm was Harry Margham who was born in 1865 at the army barracks in Dublin, his father being a sergeant in the Royal Horse Artillery. Harry moved to the Island from Southampton in 1884. Initially he worked on the construction of invalid carriages for the firm of Withams in Pyle Street, Newport and then formed a partnership with a Mr Trickett. In 1888 he started a business under his own name as a coachbuilder and wheelwright of horse-drawn vehicles quite close to the centre of Newport at 59 Crocker Street.

In 1902 Harry Margham built a new car body for a steam car. During 1911 Harry built his first van body on a Napier chassis and this was followed by other commercial vehicles for local businesses. Then in 1913 permission was granted by the Society of Motor Manufacturers to exhibit a motor vehicle at the Isle of Wight Agricultural Show at Nine Acre Field, Newport, and a body was built, providing excellent publicity for the firm.

Wagon building was still taking place at that time, a two-wheeled cart costing £14 to complete. By 1914 a four-wheeled Margham hay wagon was made, painted and sign written for £36. If the farmer required a varnish finish this added an extra £4 to the cost. All the timber for a vehicle came out of the same log and each plank was therefore very similar. After a gradual decline of the horse-drawn side of the business the final set of wooden cart shafts was produced in 1953.

In 1921 the company built their first open charabanc body and this class of work gradually improved in design to the familiar types of bus and coach bodies of the 1930s. Between 1921 and 1949 Marghams built or repaired bus and coach bodies for many local operators including Fowler's Royal Blue of Cowes, Vectis Bus Company, Isle of Wight Tourist Company Ltd., Brown's Bus Service of Carisbrooke, Wavell's Enterprise Bus Service, Young's Coaches, Coombes Brothers, Lane's Motor Tours, Pink Brothers, Coopers of Freshwater, Walkden's Bus Service, Moss Motor Tours, Shotters Ltd. of Brighstone, Southern Vectis Omnibus Company Ltd. and Holmes Saloon Coaches Ltd. of Cowes.

Harry Margham married Jane Dove shortly after he founded the firm. He and his wife lived in a house on the corner of Lugley Street and Hearn Street. They had eight children, including a son called Fred who went on to become Headmaster of Penge Grammar School in south London. Two of their sons, William and Arthur (known as Joe) joined their father's coachbuilding and repair business, and a daughter, Ethel, became the firm's book-keeper and cashier. In 1911 the company became Harry Margham and Son when William entered the business. The name of the firm was altered to Harry Margham and Sons when Arthur started working for the family business. The period from 1920 to 1950 was generally a time of expansion for the family business. In 1922 the Wagon and Horses public house in Crocker Street was acquired enabling a bigger workshop to be built. A few years later, in 1928, a large piece of additional land was purchased from Mew Langtons, the brewers, and this meant that the firm then owned an extensive site on the north side of Crocker Street with some of the frontage extending to the bottom of Hunny Hill. Further expansion of the business took place in 1930 with the purchase of two cottages on the south side of Crocker Street and this provided the opportunity for the firm to work on double deck vehicles.

Harry Margham died in 1945 and the firm became a limited company in 1946. The third generation of Margham entered the family business shortly afterwards when Don, son of William, joined the firm. He left Newport Grammar School and immediately signed up for a formal apprenticeship at Readings of Hilsea - a large coachbuilding firm in north Portsmouth employing around 200 people. This three and a half year training, broken by a period of national service, was paid for by Marghams and covered intensive practical tuition and experience in the body shop, design office, trim office, paint shop and panel shop. On returning to the Island Don soon progressed to become the acting foreman of the business and was made a Director at the age of 28.

Around 1960 Don's younger cousin Peter (Paddy), the son of Joe, joined the firm and subsequently became a Director.

According to Don Margham the firm was very skilled at the construction of bus and coach bodies but rarely made much money from this aspect of the business. Bodies were normally individually designed to be mounted on different makes of chassis and were therefore quite expensive to produce. The real profit for the firm came largely from the associated general repair and maintenance contracts with various bus and coach operators. Harry Margham

and Sons Ltd.'s biggest bus bodywork maintenance contract was with Southern Vectis. This long term contract was terminated around 1950, when Southern Vectis took their body repair work in-house.

Local transport historian Don Vincent has discovered that between 1925 and 1949 Harry Margham and Sons Ltd. built at least twenty seven single deck motor bus and coach bodies for Isle of Wight operators. These included bus and coach bodies for fourteen Dennis vehicles, bus bodies for four Guy vehicles

Dennis bus DL 4467, with Margham 26-seat body. This vehicle was delivered new to Isle of Wight Tourist Company Ltd. in 1926 and is seen here heading east along Ryde Esplanade en route for Seaview.

Marghams built the sturdy bodywork for this 26-seat Dennis E bus for Isle of Wight Tourist Co. Ltd. in 1926. Note the rather square appearance of the vehicle which was quite common for bus bodywork generally in that decade.

plus a few bodies for Star, Morris, Bristol, Commer and Daimler chassis. The bus bodies for two 35-seat Bristol L5G vehicles for Southern Vectis (CDL 614 and CDL 615) were part of a large batch of sixteen new vehicles delivered in 1939. They were constructed to standard designs provided by Eastern Coachworks Ltd. of Lowestoft, who built the bodies for the other fourteen vehicles (CDL 600 to CDL 613). The last two PSV bodies built by Harry Margham and Sons Ltd. were a 32-seat body for a Daimler CVD6 coach for Shotters Ltd. of Brighstone in 1948 (FDL 67) and a 29-seat body for a Commer Commando coach for Holmes Saloon Coaches Ltd. of Cowes in 1949 (GDL 58).

In addition to building approximately thirty new bus and coach bodies Harry Margham and Sons Ltd. were responsible for rebuilding at least nineteen bodies. The bulk of this work was carried out for Dodson Brothers Ltd. (Vectis Bus Company), Isle of Wight Tourist Company Ltd. and Southern Vectis. This was a significant area of work in the late 1940s when Marghams were responsible for modernising/ refurbishing many pre-war single deck buses for Southern Vectis, including the replacement of folding canvas roofs with fixed metal roofs.

Harry Margham and Sons Ltd. reached its peak in the late 1940s when it employed around 55 staff in its Crocker Street workshops. Production of caravans took place in the 1950s and 1960s and commercial vehicles continued to be built up to 1968 with the delivery of three flatbed lorries for Whitbreads. The business gradually diversified into car body repair and paint work and this formed the core of the firm's activities up to its centenary in 1988. This notable milestone was marked by the publication of a special illustrated supplement in the Isle of Wight County Press. The company ceased trading in 1999, having played a significant role in the Island's economy for many years. Unfortunately most of the remaining early company records and photographs were destroyed by the major floods that affected large parts of Newport on 1st October 1960. The photo below shows the extent of the flooding at Lukely Brook at the foot of Hunny Hill at that time, adjacent to Marghams' Crocker Street workshops.

Dennis Lancet DL 7990 had a 32-seat rear entrance body built by Marghams in 1932. The bus was delivered new to Brown's Bus Service. It was used by the firm until the whole business was sold to Southern Vectis in 1935. The bus is shown in St. James' Square, Newport, still working on its former route to the West Wight in the late 1930s.

Marghams built the original 30-seat body for ADL 400, a Dennis Lancet coach, in 1936. It was purchased by Isle of Wight Tourist Co. Ltd. of Ryde. From 1938 to 1952 it was a part of Southern Vectis' coaching fleet, the vehicle being rebodied shortly after the Second World War. This photograph was taken in 1949.

This photograph shows DL 8362, a Dennis Lancet coach. Marghams built the soft top body for this 30-seat vehicle which was delivered new to Isle of Wight Tourist Co. Ltd. in 1933. Originally the coach had twin front and rear entrances. After the Second World War Marghams rebodied the coach for Southern Vectis. The new body had a solid roof, a single rear entrance and two additional seats.

This handsome Bedford WTB with Margham bodywork (ADL 309) was delivered new to Isle of Wight Tourist Co. Ltd. in 1936. It was used for private hire and excursions work before being sold to Southern Vectis in 1938 along with eleven other vehicles. The coach was rebodied by Margham in 1946. These two photographs of the 26-seat vehicle were taken in July 1949, shortly before it was sold. The final Isle of Wight Tourist Co. Ltd. coach to be disposed of by Southern Vectis was another Bedford WTB with Duple bodywork (BDL 278) which was withdrawn in 1954.

The final PSV body to be built by Marghams was for GDL 58, a Commer Commando. This was a 29-seat body and the vehicle was delivered to Holmes Saloon Coaches, Ltd. of Cowes in 1949. The coach is shown at Ryde Esplanade in the late 1950s.

9 VEHICLE PHOTO GALLERY (1905 – 1945)

This clear action-packed image of the Pier Approach, Ryde Esplanade in 1905 shows three of Isle of Wight Express Motor Syndicate Ltd.'s Milnes-Daimler double deck buses plus several horse-drawn vehicles. Ryde was a very busy gateway for visitors to the Island in the early twentieth century and operators jostled for customers to various destinations as they came off the passenger ferries from Portsmouth.

A particularly clear view of the rear of DL 76, a Milnes-Daimler double deck bus. The open staircase appears almost like a ladder. This photograph was taken on the Ryde to Seaview service in 1905.

One of several popular postcards of Ryde Esplanade in 1905 shows two of the new double deck Milnes-Daimler buses competing for passengers with a number of horse-drawn vehicles.

This colour postcard of Cowes High Street, also produced around 1905, shows a bustling scene with pedestrians and various horse-drawn vehicles.

This photograph, taken on a very sunny day in 1905, shows Isle of Wight Express Motor Syndicate Ltd. Milnes-Daimler DL 78 in front of the former Royal Pier Hotel, Ryde. Several drivers and conductors stand on either side of the bus, dressed smartly in their company jackets, ties and caps. The vehicle is ready to depart on a scheduled service.

Sister Milnes-Daimler bus DL 79 pauses to be photographed outside the Porter, Carver and Gilder store in Shanklin, flanked by a crowd of local onlookers. This vehicle was in service on the Isle of Wight Express Motor Syndicate Ltd.'s route from Ryde to Shanklin via Brading and Sandown in 1905.

An Edwardian photographer captured this fine image of IWEMS Milnes-Daimler DL 79 climbing Brading High Street on its way from Ryde to Shanklin in 1905.

In 1906 the original IWEMS fleet of nine double deck buses was replaced by seven more powerful single deck Milnes-Daimler charabancs and two FIAT double deck buses. DL 130 is shown approaching Ryde St John's church, having just climbed out of the town.

UNION STREET, RYDE.

One of Isle of Wight Express Motor Syndicate Ltd.'s seven single deck Milnes-Daimler charabanc buses is seen climbing Union Street, Ryde. It was leaving the town centre in 1906 shortly after these vehicles had replaced the nine underpowered double deck Milnes-Daimlers. The photo shows the enclosed rear section of the 30-seat body which was built by Ryde coachbuilder George Mulliss and Co.

One of the batch of seven single deck Milnes-Daimler charabancs, DL 134, was fitted with a Dodson double deck body. This vehicle is shown at Freshwater Bay in a splendid Edwardian group photo. The bus is believed to have been taking staff from Messrs. Arnell Brothers, a Newport firm of millers, on an outing to the West Wight in June 1907.

THE LAST MOTOR BUS FROM RYDE, I.O.W.

Isle of Wight Express Motor Syndicate Ltd. operated a network of local bus services in the summer months of 1905, 1906 and 1907. Following the demise of the firm this humorous postcard was published, showing the scenes on the last day of service. Fifteen years were to elapse before the Island enjoyed an extensive network of motor bus services once again.

Horse-drawn coaches continued to be the main form of road passenger transport on the Isle of Wight up to around 1920. A well patronised stage coach stops to be photographed in Shanklin during a local excursion. The vehicle was capable of carrying 20 people, with external access by ladder. The image probably dates from around 1910.

One of Creeth of Nettlestone's earliest steam-powered buses was OS 41, a Darracq-Serpollet vehicle with Creeth bodywork. This bus operated on the firm's Ryde to Seaview service for several years before the First World War. It gained the nickname of "Elijah's chariot" as a result of the clouds of steam that it emitted when being refilled with water.

Facing page: DL 1824, an 18-seat Leyland charabanc, is seen passing through picturesque Shanklin Old Village in the early 1920s. This vehicle was owned by Sandown Motor Touring Company from 1920 to 1932.

This photograph, taken in the Square, Yarmouth c.1925 shows three small buses, probably all Fords, with their drivers. This was the traditional terminus for West Wight local bus services linking with the Lymington to Yarmouth ferry, adjacent to Yarmouth Pier. DL 983, the wagonette bus on the left, was a Cooper vehicle. The other two buses, both Ford T's, may have belonged to either Pink Brothers or Cooper.

Daimler W charabanc DL 1827 is one of the only two known examples of coachbuilding by F. Sivell of Ventnor. The 29-seat vehicle was operated by E.H. Crinage of Ventnor for private hire and excursions work from 1921 before being sold to A. Cooper of Freshwater for further passenger carrying service a few years later.

Another West Wight operator in the 1920s and 1930s was Pink Brothers (Freshwater and Totland Motor Bus Company). One of Pinks' early buses, probably a Ford 14-seater, is seen carrying a huge load of suitcases to the ferry at Yarmouth.

One of the first buses to be owned by Wavell's Enterprise Bus Service was a 24-seat Daimler, DL 2205, which was delivered in March 1921. The firm was based in South Street, Newport, its garage being on the site of the current Co-operative supermarket.

Three generations of the Wavell family appear in this photograph of their Ford 20-seat bus. The vehicle, registered DL 2604, had a BAICO extension and was new in April 1922. A very young Joan Kirkby (nee Wavell) is seen with her father Jack and grandfather Joseph.

For a few years in the 1920s Vectis Bus Company operated several Vulcan buses with 24-seat Dodson bodies alongside a number of larger Daimler single deck vehicles. A rare view of Vulcan DL 2906 and its crew is provided in this photograph, which was taken around 1925.

The main focus of this book is on buses but several photographs of charabancs and coaches have also been included. This fine view, taken near Alum Bay in the early 1920s, shows several charabancs owned by Coombes Brothers of Shanklin. The family business undertook private hire and excursions work to various parts of the Island from 1913 to the late 1940s. Unusually this firm also operated pleasure flights in the 1930s from a small airfield near Shanklin.

Fowler's Royal Blue (Isle of Wight Motor Service Co. Ltd.) operated a fleet of around ten Daimler buses and charabancs from Cowes in the early 1920s and were serious competitors of Wavell's Enterprise Bus Service and Vectis Bus Company. DL 3057, a sturdy 24-seat Daimler charabanc, was delivered new to the firm in May 1923.

Miss Annie Bennett ran a local bus service from Cowes to Newport via Northwood and Marks Corner from 1925 to 1926. This scarce photograph shows her bus, DL 3910, a 1925 Morris 14-seater, parked outside her grocer's shop – the former sub post office - in Pallance Road, Northwood. The small Leyland Trojan 10cwt. delivery van behind the bus (DL 3340) also belonged to Miss Bennett. Annie Bennett also owned a second bus, DL 4386, a 1925 Ford 14-seater, which was sold to Wavell's Enterprise Bus Service after a few months.

Brown's Bus Service of Carisbrooke and Totland operated this 20-seat Dennis bus in the late 1920s. Captain Joseph S. Brown ran two frequent services from Newport to the West Wight from 1925 to 1935. In 1935 the firm owned eleven buses, four of which had bodies built by Marghams in Newport.

In the East Wight Frederick Lawson's Regel Bus Service was based in Shanklin. The firm had one route from Shanklin to Ventnor and another from Sandown to Bembridge in the late 1920s and early 1930s. This picture shows "Regel" bus DL 5191, a Dennis E-type bus with a Dennis 26-seat body that was new in June 1927. The vehicle went on to give further service as a bus with Brown's Bus Service and Southern Vectis before working as a showman's caravan in South Wales up to 1948.

Alexander Harvey Hunter (Pioneer Bus Service) operated these two fourteen-seat buses on local bus services in the Ryde area in the 1920s. Ford T (NR 479) and Chevrolet X (DL 4854) are pictured with a large group of children prior to a Sunday School outing, c. 1927. Note the children's hats which mirrored the adult fashions at that time.

Albert Edward King ran several local bus services in and around Newport from 1924 to 1934. This photograph illustrates a typical King vehicle – a Chevrolet 14-seater, DL 5527, which was new in 1928. The bus is believed to have had five different Isle of Wight owners between 1928 and 1938.

A rear view of Hilton Hall's Dodge bus, DL 5709, with 20-seat Strachan and Brown bodywork. This classic "chaser" vehicle was involved in much active on-the-road competition with Brown's Bus Service on the route between Newport and the West Wight via Shalfleet and Yarmouth in the late 1920s.

DL 6767, a Ford 14-seat bus new in 1930, was owned by G.H.J. Meguyer of Sandown. Meguyer operated a local town service in and around Sandown from 1919 to the early 1950s. Much of the business involved taking holidaymakers between the railway station and their hotels.

In the early 1920s George Shotter converted his long-established horse-drawn carrier service from Brighstone to Newport to motorised vans and buses. This photograph from the mid 1920s shows one of Shotter's first motorised vehicles that carried both goods and people. It was taken in St. Thomas' Square, Newport, the traditional market town terminus for Isle of Wight carriers.

Shotters' Dennis bus (almost certainly DL 5600) is photographed with George Arthur Shotter and one of his sons, William, in St Thomas' Square Newport. The vehicle had a 20-seat Strachan and Brown body and was delivered new in 1926. It operated on the firm's service from Newport to Brighstone via Shorwell.

Between 1927 and 1929 F.W. Casey of Ryde operated in direct competition with Vectis Bus Company on the busy Ryde to Newport route via Wootton Bridge and Fairlee. The firm owned three 20-seat Guy "chasers" with swift acceleration, DL 5277/5278 (with Strachan and Brown bodywork) and DL 6220 (with Guy bodywork). The vehicle above is either DL 5277 or DL 5278. Southern Vectis bought Casey's business in 1929 and continued to operate the three small Guy buses within its fleet until 1935.

Walkden's Bus service of Sandown operated a mixed fleet of vehicles on its routes in the East Wight. DL 5585, a Morris Z with Strachan 17-seat body, was new in 1928 and was used by the firm until 1935.

These two lovely photographs of DL 7056 are believed to have been taken in Northampton by Grose Ltd., just after the bus bodywork was completed. The vehicle would have been delivered to the Island a few days later.

This very stylish 20-seat Commer Invader bus was delivered new to H. Brennan and H. Dyer (Central Bus Service) of Godshill in June 1930. It was used on the "Central" route from Newport to Shanklin via Godshill until June 1932, when the business was sold to Southern Vectis.

DL 7411, a fine 20-seat open top REO coach, was operated by Mr M.H. Caws, the owner of the Crab and Lobster Hotel, Ventnor under the trading name of "Caws' Tours". The vehicle was employed by this business on private hire and excursions work between 1931 and 1949 when it was sold to E.H. Crinage and Sons Ltd., Ventnor. Standing at the side of the vehicle was smartly dressed driver Newnes.

Two Coffen (Pioneer Bus Service) buses on Ryde local services to Haylands and Elmfield are pictured immediately behind Southern Vectis 32-seat ADC DL 5581 on the route to Newport. The photograph was taken in the early 1930s at Ryde Esplanade.

Before the Second World War Shotters' garage was located in Brighstone, where the former carriers' business was founded. This historic photograph shows the firm's fleet of buses around 1935. To the right of the photo is DL 9065, a 20-seat Dennis Ace bus which had been delivered new in 1934. After fourteen years of active service with Shotters the vehicle was sold to Meguyer of Sandown. Two years later the small bus was sold again to Nash of Ventnor where it worked for a further five years on the Ventnor town service.

A Colsons' 20-seat Dennis bus, DL 5797, ahead of two Southern Vectis buses in St. James' Square, Newport, where most local bus services terminated until the 1950s. This photograph was taken in the late 1930s. The double deck Dennis Lance bus was one of Southern Vectis' six earliest vehicles of this type. These buses were new in 1936 more than thirty years after Isle of Wight Express Motor Syndicate Ltd. brought the first double deck buses to the Island.

10 DECLINE UP TO THE MID-1950s

From 1929 several factors in combination led to the steady decline of the previously vibrant independent bus sector from twenty five firms to just one in 1957.

The formation of the Southern Vectis Omnibus Company Ltd. in 1929

In a major move that mirrored similar railway company business acquisitions around the country at that time the Southern Railway purchased 50% of the share capital of Vectis Bus Company from the Dodson Brothers in 1929. Vectis Bus Company had become the largest bus operator on the Island with over thirty single deck vehicles. With a big influx of new capital from the mainland it became a much more powerful company with ambitions to dominate the supply of bus services for local residents and visitors. Southern Railway shareholders realised the potential for large profits that could be made in the complementary Isle of Wight road passenger transport market. A well-resourced and highly competitive Southern Vectis (named after both the Southern Railway and Vectis Bus Company) was seen as the means of achieving this strategic commercial objective.

The Road Traffic Act 1930

During the 1920s lightly regulated on-the-road competition between bus operators had undoubtedly led to a number of traffic and passenger safety issues which needed to be addressed. The 1930 Road Traffic Act was a very important piece of legislation which had a profound impact on the provision of bus and coach services in the UK for the next fifty years. Essentially the Act introduced a comprehensive system of regulation for this whole area of passenger transport. Individual road service licences had to be obtained for each stage carriage, express or excursion operation, PSV licences were needed to ensure the roadworthiness of each bus and all drivers and conductors had to be officially licensed. Area Traffic Commissioners were created and they became responsible for issuing road service licences for proposed new bus routes. When applying for such licences operators had

to demonstrate that the additional service was required. Other interested parties were entitled to object to new routes and the Traffic Commissioners were required to consider any objections before making their decisions.

The effect of the legislation was to favour the larger, better-resourced bus companies at the expense of the smaller independent firms which were generally less able to complete the necessary paperwork, to represent their cases at formal meetings or to object to proposed new routes put forward by other operators. Competition switched away from the previous on-the-road commercial battles to a more indirect off-the-road competition via the route licensing process. From 1930 onwards very few new local bus services were introduced on the Isle of Wight by independent operators. Firms worked extremely hard to continue operating their existing established services in the face of constant pressure from Southern Vectis to acquire their businesses, especially their precious route licences. Against the odds some independent operators such as Colson Brothers, Enterprise, Shotters Ltd., Seaview Services Ltd. and Blake's Bus Service continued to do quite well on their routes by maintaining the loyalty of their regular passengers.

Further change of ownership of Southern Vectis in 1932

The Dodson brothers retired in 1932 selling their remaining 50% of shares in Southern Vectis to Tilling & British Automobile Traction Ltd. This provided even greater resources and operating power to the growing bus company. The Southern Railway retained its 50% interest in the company. Walter Budd, previously the manager of Southdown's operations in the Portsmouth area, became the new General Manager at this time.

Steady increase in car ownership

In addition to having to face increased competition and work within a more regulated environment independent operators experienced a gradual reduction in demand as people bought their own cars and needed to make fewer journeys by bus. The trend was

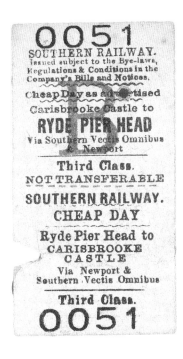

exacerbated in the 1950s by other technological developments, such as the rapid spread of television ownership. This greatly reduced the demand for evening bus travel to the Island's cinemas.

Closure of several railways in the 1950s

The closure of the branch lines from Merstone to Ventnor West (13th September 1952), Brading to Bembridge (20th September 1953), Newport to Freshwater (20th September 1953) and Newport to Sandown (5th February 1956) resulted in a further erosion of potential bus passengers for independent operators providing local railway feeder services. In addition, these rail closures provided an additional stimulus (if such stimulus were needed) for Southern Vectis to gain full control of bus services that followed the train lines that were about to disappear by acquiring any remaining competitors and their route licences.

Island-wide route network, special ticketing schemes and timetables

As Southern Vectis developed a comprehensive Island-wide network of local bus services it became even more difficult for other operators to compete with the choice of routes and attractive rover tickets that they could offer across the whole county. The firm was increasingly able to project itself as the Isle of Wight bus company rather than one of many Isle of Wight bus companies. Simultaneously, at a local level the firm was able to exploit its close working relationship with Southern Railway to sell combined rail/bus tickets to selected popular destinations. A good example of this practice is shown by the day ticket above, from Ryde to Carisbrooke Castle via Newport. These tickets were sold to visitors as they arrived on the Island at Ryde Rier Head

station and gave Southern Vectis a huge competitive advantage over firms like Colson Brothers and Shotters on the lucrative Newport to Carisbrooke bus route. Well-produced, Island-wide timetable booklets were another effective means for Southern Vectis to attract and retain additional bus passengers.

Bus station and terminal facilities

By investing in major bus stations at the key ferry ports and transport interchanges such as Ryde, Newport and Shanklin Southern Vectis obtained another significant commercial advantage over independent operators, who had to use the best possible street locations for their main bus stops. This was a key component in achieving the company's strategic objective to secure a high proportion of visitor traffic on its local bus services.

The Solent factor

The Solent acted as an effective barrier to independent bus operators setting up any additional local services in the adjoining county of Hampshire. Conversely this factor also prevented mainland-based operators from establishing new bus services on the Island. The key effect was probably to protect Southern Vectis from external competition and thus enable it to focus more rigorously on competing with and acquiring the smaller local firms.

Between 1929 and 1939 Southern Vectis pursued a strategic and relentless expansionist policy on the Island and managed to acquire fourteen independent operators of local bus services (see Appendix 3). Despite their best efforts it was extremely difficult for the smaller firms to compete effectively with their much larger, externally-funded rival in the new strictly regulated environment. One by one they felt compelled to sell their route licences, vehicles and other assets. Sometimes Southern Vectis agreed to employ members of staff of their former independent competitors. In addition they sometimes continued to run some of the re-liveried second hand buses on their previous owners' routes for several years (e.g. Brown's Bus Service from Newport to Yarmouth, Walkden's Bus Service from Shanklin to Ryde and Colson Brothers' route from Newport to Carisbrooke and Gunville).

In another similar case Herbie Wheeler, who had acquired the Newtown and Porchfield to Newport service from Brown's Bus Service in 1929, sold the route licence to Southern Vectis in 1935. Wheeler had originally started working as a carrier, taking over Mr Huggins' daily service from Newtown and Porchfield to Newport in 1925. After operating his own 'lorry bus' service for six years with his 'Flying Emmett' DL 6453, a Chevrolet 14-seater - part of which was boarded off for carriage of goods and livestock - he became the regular bus driver on the same rural route for his new employer. He is believed to have carried out this role for a further fifteen to twenty years from his home in Porchfield with an outstationed 20-seat Dennis Ace. His work also included regular school transport duties from the district to Shalfleet following the closure of the Locks Green village school. A photo of one of these vehicles, DL 9015, is shown above. This bus, which was owned by Southern Vectis from 1934 to 1959, has survived into preservation and has recently been restored to its original condition and livery.

OPERATOR CASE STUDY:
BLAKE'S BUS SERVICE, NEWPORT (1928 – 1951)

Name of firm:
1. Henry Blake (Blake's Bus Service)
2. H. & E.N. Blake (Blake's Bus Service)
3. H., E.N., H.W.N. and P.V. Blake (Blake's Bus Service)

Origin of business: Mr Blake senior (old Harry) bought the firm from Mr. Cyril Cooke of Newchurch who operated the Newport to Sandown route via Newchurch with an old model T Ford bus from 1923 to 1928. Mr Blake senior had previously worked as a carpenter for Mew Langton's brewery in Newport. Following the sale of his business Mr Cooke is believed to have emigrated to South Africa.

Nature of business: Operator of a single local bus service. Unusually, Blake's Bus Service also carried a wide variety of parcels, farm produce and small animals (e.g. bound calves), and was effectively a joint bus operator and carrier. A limited amount of private hire work was carried out on Sunday afternoons (e.g. Sunday School outings).

Location of garage: Hillside, Fairlee, Newport

Livery of vehicles: Dark brown and cream

The vehicles: The main bus for twenty years was a 14-seater Ford, registration number DL 6998 (see photo on page 108). This vehicle was new to Blake's Bus Service in June 1930 and last licensed to June 1950. The entrance for passengers was at the front, adjacent to the driver's seat. The door was opened and closed by the driver by means of a lever. There were eight forward-facing seats at the front and six inward-facing seats at the back, with a large luggage rack on the roof. It is known that DL 6998 was rebodied at least once during its long working life. A second 14-seater bus was owned (possibly Cyril Cooke's old Ford) which was kept as a spare and rarely used. In addition there was a small 8-seater "pup" vehicle which was used mainly to supplement DL 6998 on Tuesdays and Saturdays.

Bus route (Newport to Sandown via Newchurch)
St. Thomas' Square, High Street, Snook Hill, Staplers Road, Long Lane, Downend, Arreton, turn left at Branstone Cross, Newchurch, Langbridge (turn round just past railway), back through Newchurch to Winford Cross, turn left to Winford village, right hairpin bend then on to Apse Heath, turn left onto the main road to Lake, turn left towards Sandown, turn right into Beachfield Road (now one-way), drop passengers opposite junction with Pier Street. The Sandown departure point was in Melville Street, just round the corner of the junction with Beachfield Road. Buses were not permitted to pick up passengers for Newport or Sandown on the main road section of route between Arreton and Lake. These people were served by the Enterprise service that followed main roads from Shide to Sandown.

Approx. daily timetable (Monday to Friday)
(From Andrew Groves' memory)

Depart Newport 8.00am	Arrive Newchurch 8.30am
	Arrive Sandown 9.00am
Depart Sandown 10.00am	Arrive Newchurch 10.30am
	Arrive Newport 11.00am
Depart Newport 1.00pm	Arrive Newchurch 1.30pm
	Arrive Sandown 2.00pm
Depart Sandown 4.00pm	Arrive Newchurch 4.30pm
	Arrive Newport 5.00pm

On Saturdays an additional return journey would operate as follows:

Depart Newport 5.15pm	Arrive Newchurch 5.40pm
	Arrive Sandown 6.00pm
Depart Sandown 8.30pm	Arrive Newchurch 8.50pm
	Arrive Newport 9.15pm

This would enable people from the Newchurch/ Winford area to go to see the early evening film at Sandown.

There was no bus service on Sundays. Residents of Newchurch could travel to Newport and Sandown by train until 1956 when this rural branch line closed.

This photograph was taken on the Pyle Street side of St. Thomas' Square, Newport, probably around 1935. Blake's 14-seater Ford bus DL 6998 is in the centre of the picture. The presence of several vans, parcels and shop assistants provides a vivid image of the multiplicity of carrier activities that took place at this location up to 1960.

Closure of firm: The business, including the Newport to Sandown via Newchurch route was sold to Mr Jack Wavell's Enterprise Bus Service of South Street, Newport, in February 1951. Wavell continued to run the service until 18th June 1951 when Southern Vectis acquired Enterprise Bus Service's two routes from Newport to Sandown.

Shelagh Gaylard's memories

As a girl Shelagh Gaylard often visited and stayed with her grandparents in Knighton where her grandfather, George Buckett, was the superintendent of the waterworks. She remembers making many trips on Blake's Bus Service (known affectionately as 'Blakey's Bus' by local residents) from Langbridge to Sandown with her aunt. As far as she can recall the buses made relatively few trips each way per day and were well patronised for a variety of shopping and leisure trips (e.g. spending a day on the beach at Sandown). Parcels and small animals were also carried and villagers put a red flag outside their house if they wanted Mr Blake to deliver a parcel or do some shopping for them (the traditional system used by carriers). It was normally possible for children to get a seat, or sit on an adult's lap if the bus was full.

Shelagh Gaylard recalls catching the bus back from Sandown from Melville Street. The main driver in the late 1940s was Peter Blake (son of young Harry) who had a distinctive handlebar moustache and curly hair and wore a thin brown knee length coat. There was normally very little traffic on the roads. One particular memory was that the bus sometimes experienced difficulty negotiating the hairpin bend in the Winford Road near Newchurch. She also remembers the driver having to make a lot of gear changes when conveying a heavy load of passengers and parcels out of Sandown, particularly on the steep hill west of Lake on the road to Apse Heath.

Andrew Groves' memories

Andrew Groves, a cousin of Shelagh Gaylard, was brought up in Newchurch and has very strong recollections of Blake's Bus Service in the 1940s. He used the bus on many occasions to go to Sandown and Newport, and described the full route in detail. (See above). The family firm was run by three generations of the Blake family – Henry Blake senior (old Harry), Henry Blake junior (young Harry) and Peter Blake (young Harry's son). All three drove the buses at different times between 1928 and 1951. Young Harry was probably the most active partner over the years. He was an excellent motor mechanic and ensured that the main bus (DL 6998) normally ran very reliably all year round. Peter joined the firm after serving in the RAF during the Second World War. He had a military appearance with a handlebar moustache and went on to work for the Isle of Wight Fire Brigade.

Andrew Groves remembered that Blake's 14-seater bus was often well used by residents of Newchurch and Winford and sometimes carried far in excess of 20 passengers (possibly more than 40 adults and children on rare occasions). The Blakes tried not to turn any passengers away. The driver would sometimes wait for a short while outside customers' houses to receive instructions for goods to be delivered or bought in Sandown or Newport. Fares were collected by the driver as passengers entered the bus. Mr Groves did not recall any tickets being issued. The return child fare from Newchurch to Sandown was 4d.

Andrew Groves' special memories

One Saturday evening Blake's bus had a puncture outside Andrew Groves' parents' house in Newchurch around 9.00pm. Several passengers were allowed to remain sitting on the bus while Mr Blake changed the tyre. The journey to Newport was then completed.

Blakes sometimes used TVO (tractor vaporising oil) – similar to paraffin – to fuel their buses when petrol was scarce.

The remaining nine independents (Bartlett of Shanklin, Blake's Bus Service of Newport, Coopers of Freshwater, Enterprise Bus Service of Newport, Meguyer of Sandown, Nash (Brown's Bus) of Ventnor, Pink Brothers of Totland Bay, Seaview Services Ltd. and Shotters of Brighstone) continued to operate during the Second World War, albeit with major difficulties such as petrol rationing and shortages of vehicles, drivers and spare parts. Seaview Services Ltd. unusually were permitted to buy two new Bedford OWB buses with spartan 'utility' bodywork during the war because of the national importance of maintaining a regular link between Ryde and the holiday camps at Puckpool that were used for military training.

In 1946 Coopers and Pink Brothers merged to form the West Wight Motor Bus Company and continued to run several local bus services between Yarmouth, Freshwater and Alum Bay for a further six years. In February 1951 Blake's Bus Service sold its Newport to Sandown via Newchurch route licence to Wavell's Enterprise Bus Service. Enterprise then proceeded to run two local bus services between Newport and Sandown for a few months. Between June 1951 and June 1956 Southern Vectis resumed its acquisition programme and bought the route licences of Enterprise (Newport to Sandown), the West Wight Motor Bus Company, Bartlett's (Luccombe to Shanklin), Shotters Ltd. (Newport to Compton Bay and Newport to Gunville) and finally Nash's Ventnor town service. It also purchased six buses from Enterprise. These included two 56-seat double deck Guy Arab buses that were used for a further four years and an almost new Bedford OB with unusual 30-seat Duple bus bodywork (GDL 226) that provided sterling service until it was withdrawn in 1963. This left Seaview Services Ltd. as the sole remaining independent operator with its busy Ryde to Seaview route, which it would continue to operate with double deck and large single deck vehicles until 1992.

Seaview Services Ltd.'s lowbridge Leyland PD2 GDL 764 is shown ascending Union Street, Ryde. This iconic vehicle operated on the firm's long-established Ryde to Seaview local bus service for over 20 years up to 1971.

11 VEHICLE PHOTO GALLERY (1946 – 1986)

Production of buses for civilian use was extremely limited during the Second World War and "utility" bodywork was made to basic standards of design and materials. Very few new buses were delivered on the Isle of Wight between 1940 and 1945. Seaview Services Ltd. was given special permission to purchase two Bedford OWB buses in 1944 for its Ryde to Seaview route to enable soldiers to travel between Ryde and the temporary wartime base at Puckpool and St. Clare holiday camps. One of these vehicles, DDL 662, with its angular bodywork and slatted wooden seats, is shown in this photograph which was taken in the early 1950s.

Bedford OB bus GDL 226. New to Enterprise Bus Service in 1949 this vehicle worked on many rural Island routes for a total of fourteen years.

Walkden's Bus Service of Sandown operated several routes in the East Wight from 1925 to 1936, when the business (including eight buses) was sold to Southern Vectis. One of these vehicles, DL 9086, a 26-seat Leyland Cub was still in service in Sandown with its second owner until 1951. This photograph was taken in July 1949.

Most buses with more than 20 seats had a driver and conductor up to the 1960s when one-person-operation became the norm. A typical internal view of an early post-war single deck bus is illustrated above. The conductress is collecting fares and issuing tickets. She would also have been responsible for ensuring that passengers boarded and alighted from the bus safely before giving the driver the signal to proceed.

Wavell's Enterprise Bus Service had a fleet of around ten single deck and double deck buses in 1950. The firm owned several rear entrance Dennis Lancet buses, including AVW 453 which is seen in St. James' Square, Newport in July 1949.

This rare image of Enterprise Bus Service's pair of Guy Arab double deck buses with wartime utility bodywork (BRD 754 and BRD 816) was taken in South Street, Newport in 1950, outside the entrance to the firm's centrally-located garage. The buses were used on Jack Wavell's established local bus service from Newport to Sandown via Shide and Arreton until June 1951 when the business was sold reluctantly to Southern Vectis. The vehicles continued to be used on the Island until 1955.

Enterprise's Dennis Lancet WN 8981 waits in Sandown to pick up passengers on the service to Newport on 26th July 1949. Note the distinctive Enterprise bus stop that marked the Sandown terminus of this route.

Enterprise's route terminated outside the Sandown Hotel in Avenue Road, Sandown, two minutes walk from the beach. Dennis Lancet AJH 870 is waiting to set off from Sandown on its journey to Newport, also on 26th July 1949.

One of only four independent operators to survive to the mid 1950s was Bartletts of Shanklin. This small firm had operated a short local bus service from Shanklin to Luccombe Common for many years. JAL 592 was a Bedford OB, a type of vehicle that was very popular with both bus and coach operators on the Isle of Wight in the 1940s and 1950s.

Another Bartletts' bus was this Commer, registration number FCG 388. The company livery was post box red and cream. This photograph was taken on Shanklin Esplanade in the early 1950s.

After the Second World War Shotters continued to use St. Thomas' Square as the terminus for its service to Brighstone and Compton Bay (one of the best sandy beaches on the Island). Here Daimler FDL 63, one of a pair of these vehicles bought new in 1948, waits for passengers to board. Shotters ran this service until May 1956.

Nash's Dennis Ace DL 9065 was photographed in Ventnor High Street on the Ventnor Town Service in the early 1950s. Note the destination display "to and from the station". The bus did not follow a fixed route. Drivers varied the local roads and places served in and around Ventnor depending on the needs of passengers.

For a few years in the late 1950s Seaview Services Ltd operated three double deck buses on its route from Ryde to Seaview. To supplement its two famous Leyland PD2 double deck buses the firm purchased a 57-seat pre-war AEC Regent from Rochdale Corporation in 1954, registration number CDK 209. The bus was photographed at Ryde Esplanade.

Another view of Shotters' Daimler bus FDL 63 in St. Thomas' Square, in front of St. Thomas' church and Charter House. This photograph was probably taken around 1954.

In 1964 Seaview Services Ltd. purchased a 54-seat triple-axled Bedford VAL with unusual Duple/ Willowbrook bus bodywork. This vehicle (ADL 321B) was used intensively alongside double deck Leyland GDL 764 until 1971. The bus was a familiar sight between Ryde and Seaview in the late 1960s and throughout the 1970s.

GDL 764, one of the famous pair of Seaview Services Ltd.'s 53-seat Leyland PD2s from 1950, has been preserved and may sometimes be seen at the Isle of Wight Bus and Coach Museum. This lowbridge double deck vehicle has an unusual seating arrangement on the upper deck, with a sunken passenger gangway on the right hand side of six rows of seats.

Another preserved Isle of Wight vehicle is CDL 792, a Bedford OB coach with sunshine roof. Built in 1939 it was mainly employed on round-the-Island tour duties. It is painted in the firm's pre-war livery of Burma brown and cream. After the war Shotters changed its livery to post box red and dark cream.

West Wight Bus Company of Totland Bay operated several local bus routes between Freshwater, Yarmouth and Alum Bay, plus round-the-island tours with a very varied fleet. GDL 59 was a Dennis Falcon, new in 1949.

This fine AEC Regal of the West Wight Bus Company (ATO 209) was photographed at Rydc Esplanade.

H 4198
WEST WIGHT
Omnibus Co.
FRESHWATER

IN		OUT
1		10
2		9
3		8
4		7
5		6
6		5
7		4
8		3
9		2
10		1

Another view of Nash's (Brown's Bus) Dennis Ace DL 9065. The photograph was taken outside Ventnor railway station which was located about a mile from the town centre and beach.

12 A POSITIVE POSTSCRIPT

In the late 1950s, 1960s and 1970s Seaview Services Ltd. soldiered on as the sole independent operator of a local bus service on the Isle of Wight. The firm continued to provide a frequent daily service between Ryde and Seaview with a combination of Leyland double deck and Bedford single deck vehicles. Although the small operator's existence seemed relatively secure in the short term it appeared that it was only a question of time before Southern Vectis would obtain a complete monopoly over scheduled bus services throughout the county.

On 20th January 1975, however, the Royal Mail began operating Post Bus services between Newtown, Brighstone and Newport. This was part of a national network of routes that were supported by the Rural Development Commission. Using bright red and yellow Commer minibuses the Royal Mail provided a basic daily public transport service for some of the Island's most rural communities in combination with local mail collections. These two post bus routes were operated reliably for 13 years until they were withdrawn in 1988 (see page 128).

The Newport·Newtown Royal Mail Postbus

Carisbrooke Castle

One of the original Isle of Wight fleet of Commer post buses is seen here in front of Carisbrooke Castle. It was operating in the late 1970s on the Newtown to Newport route, one of the two very rural services on the Island that carried passengers and mail.

This photograph shows the first Gange's bus on the new independent service from Cowes to Ryde via Northwood and Newport, immediately prior to departure on 27th October 1986. The Mercedez vehicle was standing alongside a Southern Vectis Ford transit minibus adjacent to the Red Jet ferry terminal. There was to be very fierce competition between the two operators over the following two years. This included a landmark decision from the Office for Fair Trading that Gange vehicles should be permitted to use the Southern Vectis bus station in Newport, subject to departure fees being paid.

Then, after more than 50 years of strict regulation, the government introduced a piece of legislation which would have a profound impact on the future provision of local bus services in the UK. The 1985 Transport Act led to the deregulation of bus services outside London and to the privatisation of the National Bus Company and its subsidiary companies, including Southern Vectis. Under this new legal framework bona fide bus operators no longer had to obtain route licences to run particular services. If operators wished to operate a commercial route (i.e. without public subsidy) they simply had to register the service with the Traffic Commissioners, providing six weeks notice. Independent operators, who had been virtually excluded from setting up additional services for many years, were therefore able to take advantage of some new business opportunities.

On the Island deregulation came into effect on 26th October 1986, following a period of around twelve months when local authorities were able to ensure that certain socially necessary services were provided in addition to the commercial services that had been registered by various bus operators. Several independent operators started operating new routes in direct competition with Southern Vectis. Some of the main entrants to the market were Gange's Minicoaches of Cowes, who set up a service from Cowes (Pontoon) to Ryde Esplanade via Newport, Wiltax of Shanklin, Moss Motor Tours of Sandown (Blue Ferret) and Seaview Services Ltd. who introduced an additional route from Ryde to Sandown via Bembridge under the trading name of RedLynx.

The author was one of a handful of people on Gange's first journey from Cowes to Ryde via Newport on a Mercedes midibus on Monday 27th October 1986. (see photo on previous page) He then proceeded to catch a Seaview Services Ltd. (RedLynx) bus from Ryde to Sandown via Bembridge. (See photo below). From a passenger's point of view it was exciting that an element of competition had been restored to the local transport market.

Seaview Services Ltd. finally sold its route licence from Ryde to Seaview to Southern Vectis in 1992. Several other independent firms and Isle of Wight Council's Wight Bus have provided commercial or socially necessary local bus services after 1986. A separate book is needed to examine these recent developments in more detail.

The end! This view of the rear of a preserved 20-seat Dennis Ace was taken outside the Isle of Wight Bus and Coach Museum in October 2010. There were about 16 Dennis Ace buses and coaches working on the Isle of Wight between 1934 and the early 1960s, many with independent bus operators. Fortunately one of these vehicles, DL 9015, has recently been fully restored.

APPENDIX 1 – INDEPENDENT OPERATORS OF LOCAL BUS SERVICES (1904 – 1956)

BARNES, Clifford Vernon (Enterprise), Niton 1922 – c.1927 (L,E,P)

BARTLETT, Mrs. Mary, Shanklin, later W.W. BARTLETT (Bartlett's Garage), later J.H. & W.C. WADHAM (Wadham Bros.), inc. as BARTLETT'S GARAGE LTD. (1950) 1913 – 1956 (L,E,P) *Luccombe to Shanklin*

BARTON, Arthur Thomas, Newport 1920 - ? (L,P)

BENNETT, Miss Annie, Northwood 1925 – 1926 (L) *Cowes to Newport via Northwood*

BLAKE, Henry (Blake's Bus Service), Newport, later H. & E.N. BLAKE (Blake's Bus Service), later H., E.N., H.W.N. & P.V. BLAKE (Blake's Bus Service) 1928 – 1951 (L) *Newport to Sandown via Newchurch*

BLUNDELL, Stanley Whitaker Moss, Shanklin 1920 - ? (L,E,P)

BOXALL, F. & Sydney P., Godshill 1925 – c.1929 (L) *Newport to Sandown via Godshill and Shanklin*

BROWN, Capt. Joseph S. & Cecil A. (Brown's Bus Service), Carisbrooke, later Capt. J.S. & C.A. BROWN and William J. KEMPSTER (Brown's Bus Service) 1925 – 1935 (L,P) *Freshwater and District to Newport via several routes; Yarmouth to Alum Bay*

BROWN, Mrs. Millicent (Brown's Bus), Ventnor 1924 – by 1937 (L) *Ventnor town service from stations*

BULLOCK, Barton Henry (Surprise Bus Service), Havenstreet 1926 – 1929 (L) *Ryde to Newport via Havenstreet*

CASEY, F.W., Ryde 1927 – 1929 (L,E) *Ryde to Newport via Binstead and Wootton Bridge*

COFFEN, Charles Alfred (Pioneer Bus Service); Ryde & District Motor Service), Ryde 1931 – 1937 (L) *Ryde to Elmbridge and Ryde to Haylands*

COLSON, Frederick Arthur & Alexander (Colson Brothers), Carisbrooke, later F.A. & A. COLSON (Colson Bros), later F.A. COLSON (Colson Bros) 1920 – 1939 (L,E,P) *Newport to Carisbrooke and Gunville*

COOKE, E. Cyril, Newchurch c.1923 – 1928 (L) *Newport to Sandown via Newchurch*

COOPER, Alfred, Freshwater, later H.A., I.P., W.E. & L.B. COOPER c.1920 – 1946 (L,E,P) *Various local services between Freshwater, Yarmouth and Totland Bay*

CREETH, Arthur Herbert & Sons (Premier Motor Service), Nettlestone 1909 – 1930 (L,P) *Ryde to Seaview*

DAISH, J.E.R. (White Star), Newport by 1927 - ? *Chale/ Blackgang to Newport via Chillerton*

DALLIMORE, Louis James, Bembridge by 1928 - ? *Bembridge to Sandown*

DODSON & CAMPBELL LTD., (Vectis Bus Company), Somerton, Cowes, reincorporated as DODSON BROTHERS LTD. (Vectis Bus Company) (1922), reincorporated as THE SOUTHERN VECTIS OMNIBUS COMPANY LTD. (1929), later of Newport 1921 – date (L,E,P,D,W)

FOWLER, G. & CO., (Royal Blue), Cowes, reincorporated as I.W. MOTOR SERVICE COMPANY LTD. (Royal Blue) (1922), reincorporated as FOWLERS (I.W.) LTD. (by 1931), later B.C.F. BOLWELL (Fowler's Royal Blue Motor Coaches), Lake (1932) 1921 – c.1939 (L,E,P) *Cowes to Newport and Newport to Ventnor 1921 – c.1927*

HALL, Hilton Herbert (West Wight Bus Service), Freshwater 1927–1931 (L) *Freshwater to Newport via Yarmouth*

HAYLES, Albert James and VANNER, Mrs. A.G.H. (Supreme Bus Service), Ryde 1929 – 1933 (L)

HAYLES, O.A. (Central Bus Service), Godshill, later Harry BRENNAN and Hilton DYER (Central Bus Service), later Hilton DYER (Central Bus Service) 1925 – 1932 (L)

HINTON'S ROYAL SPA HOTEL (SHANKLIN) LTD., Shanklin by 1927 – 1938? (L)

HUNTER, Alexander Harvey (Pioneer Bus Service), Wootton, later Ryde 1924 – 1931 (L,P) *Ryde to Elmbridge and Ryde to Haylands*

ISLE OF WIGHT EXPRESS MOTOR SYNDICATE LTD., Ryde 1905 – 1907 (L,E,P) *Various routes: see Ch. 5*

KEMP, Edward (Enterprise Bus Service), Newport by 1925 – 1931 (in co-operation with J.H. Wavell) (L)

KING, Albert Edward, Carisbrooke 1924 – 1934 (L,P)

KNOX, Leonard & NEWBURY, Charles (Ideal Bus Service), Cowes 1927 – c.1928 (L)

LAWSON, Frederick D. (Regel Bus Service), Shanklin by 1926–1932 (L) *Bembridge-Sandown; Shanklin-Ventnor*

MATTHEWS, William (Matthews' Bus), Bembridge, later R.R. HODGE & F. CHILDS (Hodge & Childs), later R.R. HODGE (Hodge & Childs) (Bembridge & District) ? – 1939 (L) *Bembridge station to surrounding area*

MEGUYER, Mrs. M.A., Sandown, later G.H.J. MEGUYER, later M.W. MEGUYER 1919 – c.1952 (L,E,P)

MORRIS, Andrew Leslie, Billingham, later Niton, later Ventnor 1923 – by 1936 (L) *Chale to Ventnor via Niton and Whitwell; Ventnor to Lowtherville*

NASH, Gerald Kimber (Ventnor Engineering Co., later Nash's Motor Tours, later also Brown's Bus), Ventnor, later incorporated as NASH'S LUXURY COACHES LTD. 1922 – 1956 (L,E,P) *Ventnor town service*

NEWELL, Richard (Newell's Express Motor Service, later Seaview Services), Seaview, later incorporated as NEWELL'S (SEAVIEW) LTD. (1939), renamed SEAVIEW SERVICES LTD. (1942) 1922–date (L,E,P,W)

PINK, Albert Frederick and Arthur (Freshwater and Totland Bay Motor Bus Co.) (Pink Brothers), Totland Bay 1920 – 1946 (L,E,P) *Local services in Totland Bay, Freshwater and Yarmouth areas.*

PLATER, Frank (Isle of Wight Tourist Company), Ryde, later incorporated as ISLE OF WIGHT TOURIST COMPANY LTD. (1922) (L,E,P) 1921 – 1938 *Ryde to Seaview*

SHIER, W.J., Sandown, later Mrs. E. SHIER by 1931 - ? (L)

SHOTTER, George Arthur, William C. and Reginald P. (G.A. Shotter and Sons), Brighstone (L,E,P,D), later SHOTTERS LTD. (1946), Brighstone (merged with LANE'S AND DAVIES' MOTOR TOURS, Shanklin) c.1920 – 1974 *Newport to Brighstone/ Compton Bay; Newport to Carisbrooke and Gunville until 1956*

SPRAKE, William E. (The Chale Favourite), Chale Green by 1921 - ? (L,P)

SUMMERS, John Leslie (Reliance Bus Service), Newport by 1932 – 1937 (L,E,P)

VENTNOR ROAD CARS LTD., Ventnor 1913 – 1914 (L,E) *Ventnor town service from stations*

WALKDEN, R. (Walkden's Bus Service), Sandown, later F.J. WALKDEN & I. WILLIAMS (Walkden's Bus Service), later inc. as R. WALKDEN LTD. (1933) 1925 – 1936 (L) *(See Chapter 8 for route details)*

WARBURTON'S HOTEL, Newport 1904? – 1905? (L) *Newport station to Carisbrooke Castle* (to be confirmed)

WAVELL, Joseph Henry (Golden Garage), later Enterprise Bus Service, Newport (in co-operation with E. KEMP from by 1925 – by 1931), later J.H. and M.J. WAVELL, later M.J. WAVELL (Enterprise Bus Service) 1921-1951

WEEKS, George & Son, Calbourne c.1926 – by 1932 (L,P)

WEST WIGHT MOTOR BUS CO. LTD., Totland Bay 1946 – 1987 (L,E,P)

WHEELER, Herbert Edwin John, Porchfield 1929 – 1935 (L,E,P) *Newtown and Porchfield to Newport*

Key

Operator's name, business location, date started PSV operation, date ceased, type of operation, route(s)

L = local bus services, E = excursions and tours, P = private hire, W = workmen's services, D = long distance

Information drawn mainly from Patrick Hall's provisional list of Isle of Wight bus and coach operators, 1993.

Fowler's Royal Blue: Cowes to Newport and Newport to Ventnor, early 1920s

"ROYAL BLUE" MOTOR COACHES

For Comfort and Safety.

TIME TABLE from November 5th.

COWES, Pallance Road, & NEWPORT.

WEEKDAYS.

COWES	dep.	7.20	9.40	..	12.20	2.00	3.35	5.45	6.10	7.40	..
Gurnard	,,	7.30	9.50	..	12.30	2.10	3.45	6.00	..	7.50	
Pallance Road	,,	..	9.55	..	12.35	2.15	3.50	5.55	6.20	7.55	..
Marks Corner	,,	..	10.05	11.40	..	2.25	..	..	..	..	..
NEWPORT	arr.	..	10.25	12.00	12.50	2.45	4.05	..	6.35	8.10	..

NEWPORT	dep.	..	10.25	11.15	12.20	2.55	4.15	..	6.40	8.20	9S15
Marks Corner	,,	..	..	11.35	..	..	4.35	..	..	8.40	9S35
Pallance Road	,,	7.35	10.40	..	12.35	3.10	4.45	..	6.55	8.50	9S45
Gurnard	,,	7.30	10.45	..	12.40	3.15	4.50	6.00	7.05	8.55	9S50
COWES	arr.	7.45	10.55	..	12.50	3.35	5.00	6.10	7.15	9.05	10S00

SUNDAYS.

COWES	dep.	9.55	1.55	3.55	5.50	6.30	9.00
Gurnard	,,	10.05	2.00	4.00	6.00	6.35	9.10
Pallance Road	,,	10.10	2.05	4.05	..	6.40	9.15
Marks Corner	,,	..	2.15	..	..	6.50	9.25
NEWPORT	arr.	10.25	2.35	4.20	..	7.10	9.45

NEWPORT	dep.	10.50	3.00	4.30	..	7.00	9.50
Marks Corner	,,	..	..	4.50	..	7.20	10.10
Pallance Road	,,	11.05	3.15	5.00	..	7.30	10.20
Gurnard	,,	11.10	3.20	5.05	6.05	7.35	10.25
COWES	arr.	11.20	3.30	5.15	6.15	7.45	10.35

COWES, NEWPORT, GODSHILL, WHITWELL, and VENTNOR.

		WEEKDAYS.				SUNDAYS.				
COWES	dep.	12.20	3.35	6.10	7S40	..	1.55	..	6.30	..
NEWPORT	,,	1.00	4.15	6.40	8S20	..	2.50	..	7.20	..
Rookley	,,	1.15	4.30	6.55	8S35	..	3.05	..	7.35	..
Godshill	,,	1.35	4.40	7.05	8S45	..	3.15	..	7.45	..
Whitwell	,,	1.40	4.55	7.20	9S00	11.10	3.30	..	8.00	..
Niton	,,	1.50	5.05	7.30	9S10	11.20	3.40	5.00	8.10	9.10
St. Lawrence	,,	2.00	5.15	7.40	9S20	11.30	3.50	5.10	8.20	9.20
VENTNOR	arr.	2.10	5.20	7.50	9S30	11.40	4.00	5.20	8.30	9.30

VENTNOR	dep.	9.50	2.20	5.20	8S00	10.30	1.40	4.30	5.30	8.40
St. Lawrence	,,	10.00	2.30	5.30	8S10	10.40	1.50	4.40	5.40	8.50
Niton	,,	10.10	2.40	5.40	8S20	10.50	2.00	4.50	5.50	9.00
Whitwell	,,	10.20	2.50	5.50	8S30	11.00	2.10	..	6.00	..
Godshill	,,	10.35	3.05	6.05	8S45	..	2.25	..	6.15	..
Rookley	,,	10.45	3.15	6.15	8S55	..	2.35	..	6.25	..
NEWPORT	arr.	11.00	3.30	6.30	9S10	..	2.50	..	6.40	..
COWES	,,	..	5.00	7.15	10S00	..	3.30	..	7.45	..

S Saturdays only.

When Newport Market is closed, coaches will leave Quay Street (Town Hall).

All "Royal Blue" coaches are timed to connect with boats arriving at or departing from Cowes.

The times given above are those at which it is intended that Royal Blue Motor Coaches should arrive at or depart from the places indicated; but while every care is taken to ensure that these times are adhered to no guarantee of any sort is given that connections will be maintained and no responsibility can be accepted for any delays, accidents, or personal injury to any passenger. Return Tickets are issued subject to accommodation being available, and every effort is made to provide accommodation for passengers as required. Any passenger by accepting a ticket agrees to the conditions set out above. The I.W. Motor Service Co., Ltd.

"Royal Blue" Coaches give you Comfort and Safety.

W. Blake & Son, Printers, Town Lane, Newport.

BROWN'S BUS SERVICE.

Newport, Freshwater, Totland, &c., via The Bridge.

From
Sunday July 1st, 1934, until further notice.

Private Parties Catered For to all parts.

ADDRESSES—
BROWN'S BUS SERVICE, CLIFTON GARAGE, CARISBROOKE.
Telephone: Newport 400.

BROWN'S BUS SERVICE, CLAREMONT, THE AVENUE, TOTLAND.
Telephone: Freshwater 239.

VIA THE BRIDGE.

Freshwater Bay, Freshwater, Totland, Colwell Bay, Yarmouth, Carisbrooke, and Newport.

Brown's Bus Service.

Connections with boats at Yarmouth.

VIA SHALFLEET AND CRANMORE.

Week-days.

		X	X																						SO	SO	
Newport	dep.	7 5	8 0	9 25	1015	1040	1115	12 0	1 10	2 0	230	315	4 0	420	510	540	640	735	820	9 15	9 30	1010		
Carisbrooke	,,	—	—	9 30	1020	1045	1120	12 5	1 15	2 5	235	320	4 5	425	515	545	645	740	825	9 20	9 35	1015		
Shalfleet	,,	—	—	9 45	1035	11 0	1135	1220	1 30	220	250	335	420	440	530	6 0	7 0	755	840	9 35	9 50	1030		
Ningwood (H. & G.)	,,	—	—	9 50	1040	11 5	1140	1225	1 35	225	255	340	425	445	535	6 5	7 5	8 0	845	9 40	9 55	1035		
Cranmore	,,	—	—	9 52	1042	11 7	1142	1227	1 37	227	257	342	427	447	537	6 7	7 7	8 2	847	9 42	9 57	1037		
Yarmouth	,,	745	840	10 0	1050	1115	1150	1235	1 45	235	3 5	350	435	455	545	615	715	810	855	9 50	10 5	1045		
Hill Cross	,,	—	—	10 8	1058	1123	1158	1243	1 53	243	313	358	443	5 3	550	623	723	818	9 3	9 58	1013	1053		
Colwell Bay	,,	—	—	1012	11 2	1127	12 2	1247	1 57	247	317	4 2	447	5 7	554	627	727	822	9 7	10 2	1017	1057		
Totland Bay	,,	—	—	1015	11 5	1130	12 5	1250	2 0	250	320	4 5	450	510	555	630	730	825	910	10 5	1020	11 0		
Moa Place	,,	—	—	1020	1110	1135	1210	1255	2 5	255	325	410	455	515	6 0	635	735	830	915	1010	1025	11 5		
Railway Station	,,	—	—	1022	1112	1137	1212	1257	2 7	257	327	412	457	517	6 2	637	737	832	917	1012	1027	11 7		
Freshwater Bay	arr.	755	9 5	1025	1115	1140	1215	1 0	2 10	3 0	330	415	5 0	520	6 5	640	740	835	920	1015	1030	1110		

Freshwater Bay	dep.	755	840	9 25	10 5	1030	1140	1240	1 15	2 0	235	3 5	340	425	510	540	630	720	820	9 15
Railway Station	,,	758	843	9 28	10 8	1033	1143	1243	1 18	2 3	238	3 8	343	428	513	548	633	723	823	9 18
Moa Place	,,	8 0	845	9 30	1010	1035	1145	1245	1 20	2 5	240	310	345	430	515	550	635	725	825	9 20
Totland Bay	,,	8 5	850	9 35	1015	1040	1150	1250	1 25	210	245	315	350	435	520	555	640	730	830	9 25
Colwell Bay	,,	8 8	853	9 38	1018	1043	1153	1253	1 28	213	248	318	353	438	523	558	643	733	833	9 28
Hill Cross	,,	812	858	9 42	1022	1047	1157	1257	1 32	217	252	322	357	442	527	6 2	647	737	837	9 32
Yarmouth	,,	820	9 5	9 50	1030	1055	12 5	1 5	1 40	225	3 0	330	3 45	450	535	6 5	655	745	845	9 40
Cranmore	,,	828	913	9 58	1038	11 3	1213	1 13	1 48	233	3 8	338	413	458	543	613	7 3	753	853	9 48
Ningwood (H. & G.)	,,	830	915	10 0	1040	11 5	1215	1 15	1 50	235	310	340	415	5 0	545	615	7 5	755	855	9 50
Shalfleet	,,	835	920	10 5	1045	1110	1220	1 20	1 55	240	315	345	420	5 5	550	620	710	8 0	9 0	9 55
Carisbrooke	,,	850	935	1020	11 0	1125	1235	1 35	2 10	255	330	4 0	435	520	6 5	635	725	815	915	1010
Newport	arr.	855	940	1025	11 5	1130	1240	1 40	2 15	3 0	335	4 5	440	525	610	640	730	820	920	1015

X See Service via Calbourne.

Sunday Service on next page.

VIA THE BRIDGE.

Freshwater Bay, Freshwater, Totland, Colwell Bay, Yarmouth, Carisbrooke, and Newport.

Brown's Bus Service.

Connections with boats at Yarmouth.

VIA SHALFLEET AND CRANMORE.

Sundays.

Newport	dep.	9 45	1015	1110	1140	1 5	2 5	2 35	3 15	4 35	5 35	6 10	7 0	8 30	9 0	1010			
Carisbrooke	,,	9 50	1020	1115	1145	1 10	2 10	240	3 20	4 40	5 40	6 15	7 5	8 35	9 5	1015			
Shalfleet	,,	10 5	1035	1130	12 0	1 25	2 25	2 55	3 35	4 55	5 55	6 30	720	8 50	9 20	1030			
Ningwood (H. & G.)	,,	1010	1040	1135	12 5	1 30	2 30	3 0	3 40	5 0	6 0	6 35	725	8 55	9 25	1035			
Cranmore	,,	1012	1042	1137	12 7	1 32	2 32	3 2	3 42	5 2	6 2	6 37	727	8 57	9 27	1037			
Yarmouth	,,	1020	1050	1145	1215	1 40	2 40	3 10	3 50	5 10	6 10	6 45	735	9 5	9 35	1045			
Hill Cross	,,	1028	1058	1153	1223	1 48	2 48	3 18	3 58	5 18	6 18	6 53	743	9 13	9 43	1053			
Colwell Bay	,,	1032	11 2	1157	1227	1 52	2 52	3 22	4 2	5 22	6 22	6 57	747	9 17	9 47	1057			
Totland Bay	,,	1035	11 5	12 0	1230	1 55	2 55	3 25	4 5	5 25	6 25	7 0	750	9 20	9 50	11 0			
Moa Place	,,	1040	1110	12 5	1235	2 0	3 0	3 30	4 10	5 30	6 30	7 5	755	9 25	9 55	11 5			
Railway Station	,,	1042	1112	12 7	1237	2 2	3 2	3 32	4 12	5 32	6 32	7 7	757	9 27	9 57	11 7			
Freshwater Bay	arr.	1045	1115	1210	1240	2 5	3 5	3 35	4 15	5 35	6 35	7 10	8 0	9 30	10 0	1110			

Freshwater Bay	dep.	8 40	10 0	1115	1245	1 55	2 35	3 25	4 30	5 45	6 15	7 0	7 30	8 10	8 55	9 35			
Railway Station	,,	8 43	10 3	1118	1248	1 58	2 38	3 28	4 33	5 48	6 18	7 3	7 33	8 13	8 58	9 38			
Moa Place	,,	8 45	10 5	1120	1250	2 0	2 40	3 30	4 35	5 50	6 20	7 5	7 35	8 15	9 0	9 40			
Totland Bay	,,	8 50	1010	1125	1255	2 5	2 45	3 35	4 40	5 55	6 25	7 10	7 40	8 20	9 5	9 45			
Colwell Bay	,,	8 53	1013	1128	1258	2 8	2 48	3 38	4 43	5 58	6 28	7 13	7 43	8 23	9 8	9 48			
Hill Cross	,,	8 57	1057	1132	1 2	2 12	2 52	3 42	4 47	6 2	6 32	7 17	7 47	8 27	9 12	9 52			
Yarmouth	,,	9 5	1025	1140	1 10	2 20	3 0	3 45	4 55	6 5	6 40	7 25	7 50	8 35	9 20	10 0			
Cranmore	,,	9 13	1033	1148	1 20	2 30	3 10	3 55	5 6	6 13	6 48	7 33	7 58	8 43	9 28	10 8			
Ningwood (H. & G.)	,,	9 15	1035	1150	1 22	2 30	3 10	3 55	5 6	6 15	6 50	7 35	8 0	8 45	9 30	1010			
Shalfleet	,,	9 20	1040	1155	1 25	2 35	3 15	4 0	5 10	6 20	6 55	7 40	8 5	8 50	9 35	1015			
Carisbrooke	,,	9 35	1055	1210	1 40	2 50	3 40	4 15	5 25	6 35	7 10	7 55	8 20	9 5	9 50	1050			
Newport	arr.	9 40	11 0	1215	1 45	2 55	3 45	4 20	5 30	6 40	7 15	8 0	8 25	9 10	9 55	1035			

135

Freshwater, Yarmouth, Ningwood Station, and Newport.
Brown's Bus Service.
VIA CALBOURNE, NEWBRIDGE, AND THORLEY.

Week-days.

											SO		ME	SO
Newport	dep.	7 5	8 0	10 0	1145	1 0	2 15	3 50	5 15	6 30	7 10	8 10	8 45	10 0
Carisbrooke	,,	7 10	8 5	10 5	1150	1 5	2 20	3 55	5 20	6 35	7 15	8 15	8 50	10 5
Calbourne	,,	7 25	8 20	1020	12 5	1 20	2 35	4 10	5 35	6 50	7 30	8 30	9 5	1020
Newbridge	,,	7 30	8 25	1025	1210	1 25	2 40	4 15	5 40	6 55	7 35	8 35	9 10	1025
Ningwood Station	,,	7 33	8 28	1030	1215	1 30	2 45	4 20	5 45	7 0	7 40	8 40	9 15	1030
Wellow, Sun	,,	7 35	8 30	1033	1218	1 33	2 48	4 23	5 48	7 3	7 43	8 43	9 18	1033
Thorley Church	,,	7 40	8 35	1038	1223	1 38	2 53	4 28	5 53	7 8	7 48	8 48	9 23	1038
Yarmouth	,,	7 45	8 40	1045	1230	1 45	3 0	4 35	6 0	7 15	7 55	8 55	9 30	1045
Hill Cross	,,	*	8 48	*	*	*	*	*	*	*	*	*	*	*
Colwell Bay	,,	—	8 52	—	—	—	—	—	—	—	—	—	—	—
Totland Bay	,,	—	8 55	—	—	—	—	—	—	—	—	—	—	—
Moa Place	,,	—	9 0	—	—	—	—	—	—	—	—	—	—	—
Freshwater Station	,,	—	9 2	—	—	—	—	—	—	—	—	—	—	—
Freshwater Bay	arr.	—	9 5	—	—	—	—	—	—	—	—	—	—	—

		a.m.
Newport	dep.	7 5
Carisbrooke	,,	7 10
Calbourne	,,	7 25
Newbridge	,,	7 30
Ningwood St.	,,	7 33
Wellow, Sun	,,	7 35
Thorley	,,	7 40
Yarmouth	,,	7 45
Wilmingham	,,	7 50
Freshwater B.	,,	7 55
Freshwater	arr.	8 0

									SO			ME	
Freshwater Bay	dep.	—	—	—	—	—	—	—	—	—	—	—	—
Freshwater Station	,,	—	—	—	—	—	—	—	—	—	—	—	—
Moa Place	,,	—	—	—	—	—	—	—	—	—	—	—	—
Totland Bay	,,	—	—	—	—	—	—	—	—	—	—	—	—
Colwell Bay	,,	—	—	—	—	—	—	—	—	—	—	—	—
Hill Cross	,,	*	*	*	*	*	*	*	*	*	*	*	*
Yarmouth	,,	8 15	9 50	11 5	11 10	—	2 25	3 30	5 0	5 20	6 10	7 15	8 55	9 40
Thorley Church	,,	8 20	9 55	1112	1 17	2 32	3 37	5 7	5 27	6 17	7 22	9 2	9 47
Wellow, Sun	,,	8 25	10 0	1117	1 22	1 50	2 37	3 42	5 12	5 32	6 22	7 27	9 7	9 52
Ningwood Station	,,	8 27	10 2	1120	1 25	1 52	2 40	3 45	5 15	5 35	6 25	7 30	9 10	9 55
Newbridge	,,	8 30	10 5	1125	1 30	2 55	2 45	3 50	5 20	5 40	6 30	7 35	9 15	10 0
Calbourne	,,	8 35	1010	1130	1 35	2 2	2 50	3 55	5 25	5 45	6 35	7 40	9 20	10 5
Carisbrooke	,,	8 50	1025	1145	1 50	2 15	3 5	4 5	5 40	6 0	6 50	7 55	9 35	1020
Newport	arr.	8 55	1030	1150	1 55	2 20	3 10	4 15	5 45	6 5	6 55	8 0	9 40	1025

Sunday Service on next page.

Freshwater, Yarmouth, Ningwood Station, and Newport.
Brown's Bus Service.
VIA CALBOURNE, NEWBRIDGE, AND THORLEY.

Sundays.

Newport	dep.	9 45	1120	12 0	2 45	4 25	6 0	8 0	8 45	10 0
Carisbrooke	,,	9 50	1125	2 5	2 50	4 30	6 5	8 5	8 50	10 5
Calbourne	,,	10 5	1140	2 20	3 5	4 45	6 20	8 20	9 5	1020
Newbridge	,,	1010	1145	2 25	3 10	4 50	6 25	8 25	9 10	1025
Ningwood Station	,,	1015	1150	2 28	3 15	4 53	6 30	8 30	9 15	1030
Wellow, Sun	,,	1018	1153	2 30	3 18	4 55	6 33	8 33	9 18	1033
Thorley Church	,,	1023	1158	2 35	3 23	5 0	6 38	8 38	9 23	1038
Yarmouth	arr.	1030	12 5	2 40	3 30	5 5	6 45	8 45	9 30	1045

		*	*	*	*	*	*	*	*	*	*
Yarmouth	dep.	1035	1 10	3 0	4 0	5 30	7 30	8 45	10 0
Thorley Church	,,	1042	1 17	3 7	4 7	5 37	7 37	8 52	10 7
Wellow, Sun	,,	1047	1 22	3 12	4 12	5 42	7 42	8 57	1012
Ningwood Station	,,	1050	1 25	3 15	4 15	5 45	7 45	9 0	1015
Newbridge	,,	1055	1 30	3 20	4 20	5 50	7 50	9 5	1020
Calbourne	,,	11 0	1 35	3 25	4 25	5 55	7 55	9 10	1025
Carisbrooke	,,	1115	1 50	3 40	4 40	6 10	8 10	9 25	1040
Newport	,,	1120	1 55	3 45	4 45	6 15	8 15	9 30	1045

* See Main Road Service for times and connections at Yarmouth to and from Freshwater, etc.

TOTLAND BAY AND ALUM BAY.

Brown's Bus Service.

Week-days.

														SE
Totland Bay	dep.	11 5	1130	12 5	1250	2 0	2 50	3 20	4 10	4 50	5 55	7 30
Alum Bay	arr.	1110	1135	1210	1255	2 5	2 55	3 25	4 15	4 55	6 0	7 35

										SE
Alum Bay	dep.	1145	1245	2 5	3 10	3 45	4 30	5 15	5 50	6 35	7 25
Totland Bay	arr.	1150	1250	2 10	3 15	3 50	4 35	5 20	5 55	6 40	7 30

SE Saturdays excepted.

Sundays.

Totland Bay	dep.	11 5	1230	1 55	2 55	3 30	4 5	5 25	6 25	7 50
Alum Bay	arr.	1110	1235	2 0	3 0	3 35	4 10	5 30	6 30	7 55

Alum Bay	dep.	1120	1250	2 0	3 25	4 35	5 50	6 20	7 5	8 15
Totland Bay	arr.	1125	1255	2 5	3 30	4 40	5 55	6 25	7 10	8 20

The above buses connect with the Main Route buses to and from Newport, etc., at Totland.

The times given are those at which it is intended that Brown's Buses should arrive at or depart from the places indicated; but while every care is taken to ensure that these times are adhered to, no guarantee of any sort is given that connections will be maintained, nor will the proprietors be accountable for any loss, inconvenience, or injury arising from delay or detention from any cause. Return Tickets are issued subject to accommodation being available, and every effort is made to provide accommodation for passengers as required. Any passenger by accepting a ticket agrees to the conditions set out above.

Children over 4 years and under 12 years must pay half fare if standing. There is no objection to a Child using a seat if not required by a full fare passenger.

Parcels.—All Parcels must be prepaid and a ticket taken. Parcels addressed to persons on the line of route are only accepted on the distinct understanding that the Bus will be met. No responsibility whatever is accepted for delay, loss, or damage if such parcels are not met.

I.W. County Press.—1112-6-34.

SHOTTERS, LTD.

Registered Office: Moortown, Brighstone. Tel Brighstone 358.

Branch Offices: Sandown Road Coach Station, Shanklin. Tel. Shanklin 2204.
Regent Street, Shanklin. Tel. Shanklin 2201.
High Street, Sandown. Tel. Sandown 511.

TIME TABLE FROM THURSDAY 2nd JUNE—25th SEPT., 1949.

COMPTON, BROOK, BRIGHSTONE, SHORWELL, AND NEWPORT.

WEEK-DAYS.

		NBH	NBH								A		Sat.	Sat.
Compton (Huts)	dep.	—	—	—	—	1110	12 51	1 0	2 0	3 5	—	5 5	—	7 15	—
Brook (Farm)	"	7 7	8 3	9 3	9 33	1115	1210	1 52	2 53	3 10	4 45	5 10	6 20	7 20	7 50	8 50
Brighstone (Cooper's Shop)	"	7 15	8 13	9 13	9 43	1125	1220	1 15	2 15	3 20	4 55	5 20	6 30	7 30	8 09	9 0
Shorwell (Crown Inn)	"	7 22	8 23	9 23	9 53	1135	—	1 25	2 25	3 30	5 5	5 30	6 40	7 40	8 10	9 10
Carisbrooke (Vicarage)	"	7 37	8 38	9 38	10 8	1150	—	1 40	2 40	3 45	5 20	5 45	6 55	7 55	8 25	9 25
Newport (St. Thomas's Sq.)	arr.	7 42	8 43	9 43	1013	1155	—	1 45	2 45	3 50	5 25	5 50	7 0	8 0	8 30	9 30

		NBH	NBH					A	Sat.	Sat	W
Newport (St. Thomas's Sq.)	dep.	7 45	8 55	1020	120	210	2 20	3 55	4 25	5 30	6 10	7 10	8 10	8 35	9 35	1035
Carisbrooke (Vicarage)	"	7 50	9 0	1025	1125	1215	2 54	0 4	3 05	3 56	7 57	158	158	40 9	40	1040
Shorwell (Crown Inn)	"	8 5	9 15	1040	1140	1230	2 40	4 15	4 45	5 50	97	308	308	559	55	1055
Brighstone (Cooper's Shop)	"	8 1	9 2	1050	1150	1240	2 50	4 25	4 52	6 0	07	408	409	510	511	5
Brook (Farm)	"	8 30	9 11	012	0 1250	3 04	3 55	06	106	507	508	509	15	1015	—
Compton (Huts)	arr.	—	11 5	12 5	1255	3 5	—	5 5	—	6 55	—	—	—	—

Sat.—Saturdays, Whit Monday, and August Bank Holiday.   A—Saturdays, then week-days from 13th July to 9th September.
W—Wednesdays, Whit Monday, and August Bank Holiday.   NBH—Not Whit Monday or August Bank Holiday.

SUNDAYS.

Compton (Huts)	dep.	—	—	1110	1 153	5	—	5 45	7 30	8 0	—
Brook (Farm)	"	—	—	1115	1 20	3 104	5	5 50	7 35	8 5	9 20
Brighstone (Cooper's Shop)	"	9 35	1125	1 30	3 20	4 15	6 07	4 58	15	9 30
Shorwell (Crown Inn)	"	9 45	1135	1 40	—	4 25	6 10	7 55	8 25	9 40
Carisbrooke (Vicarage)	"	10 0	1150	1 55	—	4 40	6 25	8 10	8 40	9 55
St. James's Sq. arr.	10 5	1155	2 0	—	4 45	6 30	8 15	8 45	10 0

St. James's Sq. dep.	1020	1210	2 20	5 0	6 40	8 35	9 0	10 5
Carisbrooke (Vicarage)	1025	1215	2 25	5 56	6 45	8 40	9 5	1010
Shorwell (Crown Inn)	1040	1230	2 40	5 20	7 0	8 55	9 20	1025
Brighstone (Cooper's Shop)	1050	1240	2 50	5 30	7 10	9 5	9 30	1035
Brook (Farm)	11 0	1250	3 0	5 40	7 20	9 15	9 40	—
Compton (Huts) arr.	11 5	1255	5 5	45	7 25	—	—

NEWPORT, ST. JAMES'S SQUARE, CARISBROOKE, AND GUNVILLE.

		NSB	NSB	NS	NS	NS	NS	NS	NS	NS	NS	NS	NS	NS	NS	NS	NS	NS	NS	NS	NS
Gunville (Ash Lane)	dep.	7 45	8 30	9 0	9 30	10 0	1030	11 0	1130	12 0	1230	1 0	1 30	2 0	2 30	3 0	3 30	4 0	4 30	5 0	5 30	6 0	6 30	7 0	7 30	8 0	8 30
Carisbrooke (Brown's Stores)	"	7 50	8 35	9 5	9 35	10 5	1035	11 5	1135	12 5	1235	1 5	1 35	2 5	2 35	3 5	3 35	4 5	4 35	5 5	5 35	6 5	6 35	7 5	7 35	8 5	8 35
Newport (St. James's Sq.)	arr.	7 55	8 40	9 10	9 40	1010	1040	1110	1140	1210	1240	1 10	1 40	2 10	2 40	3 10	3 40	4 10	4 40	5 10	5 40	6 10	6 40	7 10	7 40	8 10	8 40

					NS
Gunville (Ash Lane)	dep.	9 0	9 30	10 0	1025
Carisbrooke (Brown's Stores)	"	9 5	9 35	10 5	1030
Newport (St. James's Sq.)	arr.	9 10	9 40	1010	1035

		NSB	NSB	NS	NS	NS	NS	NS	NS	NS	NS	NS	NS	NS	NS	NS	NS	NS	NS	NS	NS
Newport (St. James's Sq.)	dep.	8 0	8 45	9 15	9 45	1015	1045	1115	1145	1215	1245	1 15	1 45	2 15	2 45	3 15	3 45	4 15	4 45	5 15	5 45	6 15	6 45	7 15	7 45	8 15	8 45
Carisbrooke (Brown's Stores)	"	8 5	8 50	9 20	9 50	1020	1050	1120	1150	1220	1250	1 20	1 50	2 20	2 50	3 20	3 50	4 20	4 50	5 20	5 50	6 20	6 50	7 20	7 50	8 20	8 50
Gunville (Ash Lane)	arr.	8 8	8 53	9 23	9 53	1023	1053	1123	1153	1223	1253	1 23	1 53	2 23	2 53	3 23	3 53	4 23	4 53	5 23	5 53	6 23	6 53	7 23	7 53	8 23	8 53

				NS	
Newport (St. James's Sq.)	dep.	9 15	9 45	1015	1040
Carisbrooke (Brown's Stores)	"	9 20	9 50	1020	1045
Gunville (Ash Lane)	arr.	9 23	9 53	1023	1048

NS—Not Sundays.   NSB—Not Sundays, Whit Monday, or August Bank Holiday.

Every endeavour is made to ensure the regularity and punctuality of the service, but the Company hereby give notice that they will not be responsible for any loss or inconvenience arising from any delay, however caused.

ALL PARCELS MUST BE SENT CARRIAGE PAID AND MUST BE MET AT DESTINATION.

EXCURSIONS AND TOURS FROM SHANKLIN, SANDOWN, AND NEWPORT.

Day, Half-day, and Evening Tours can be booked from the Company's Offices at Regent Street, Shanklin; Sandown Road Coach Station, Shanklin; and High Street, Sandown.

PRIVATE PARTY TRAVEL – ISLAND OR MAINLAND.

Coaches for Hire: 20, 26, 29, 32, 33, and 35 seaters.

I.W. COUNTY PRESS.—594-4-49.

Shotters Ltd.: Newport to Brighstone/ Compton Bay; Newport to Gunville, 2nd June to 25th September 1949

ENTERPRISE BUS SERVICE
TIME TABLE

(From 25th September until further notice).

WEEK-DAYS.

Newport	dep.	730	915	1015	1115	1215	115	215	315	355	435	515	555	730	9 0
Arreton P.O.	,,	745	930	1030	1130	1230	130	230	330	410	450	530	610	745	915
Apse Heath	,,	755	940	1040	1140	1240	140	240	340	420	5 0	540	620	755	925
Lake	,,	8 0	945	1045	1145	1245	145	245	345	425	5 5	545	625	8 0	930
Sandown	arr.	8 5	950	1050	1150	1250	150	250	350	430	510	550	630	8 5	935

Sandown	dep.	810	10 8	11 8	12 8	1 8	2 8	3 8	355	435	515	555	635	810	940
Lake	,,	815	1013	1113	1213	113	213	313	4 0	440	520	6 0	640	815	945
Apse Heath	,,	820	1018	1118	1218	118	218	318	4 5	445	525	6 5	645	820	950
Arreton P.O.	,,	830	1028	1128	1228	128	228	328	415	450	535	610	655	830	955
Newport	arr.	845	1043	1143	1243	143	243	343	430	5 5	550	625	710	845	1010

BOXING DAY—SUNDAY SERVICE.   **CHRISTMAS DAY—NO SERVICE.**

SUNDAYS.

Newport	dep.	1020	1140	115	215	3 0	415	515	630	745	9 0
Arreton P.O.	,,	1035	1155	130	230	315	430	530	645	8 0	915
Apse Heath	,,	1040	12 0	140	240	320	435	540	650	8 5	920
Lake	,,	1045	12 5	145	245	325	440	545	655	810	925
Sandown	arr.	1050	1210	150	250	330	445	550	7 0	815	930

Sandown	dep.	11 0	1215	2 8	3 8	335	450	555	7 5	820	935
Lake	,,	11 5	1220	213	313	340	455	6 0	710	825	940
Apse Heath	,,	1110	1225	218	318	345	5 0	6 5	715	830	945
Arreton P.O.	,,	1115	1230	228	328	350	5 5	610	720	835	950
Newport	arr.	1130	1245	243	343	4 5	520	625	735	850	10 5

FARES.

Newport, St. James's Square									Where the Single Fare is	Return Fare is
2	**Shide**								3d.	5d.
3	2	**Blackwater**							4d.	7d.
5	3	2	**Merstone X**						5d.	8d.
6	5	3	2	**Arreton**					6d.	9d.
7	6	4	3	2	**Hale Common**				7d.	1/-
8	7	5	4	3	2	**Branstone**			8d.	1/2
9	8	6	4	4	3	2	**Apse Heath**		9d.	1/3
10	9	8	5	4	4	3	2	**Merry Gardens**	10d.	1/4
10	9	8	6	5	4	3	2	2 **Lake P.O.**	1/-	1/6
1/-	10	9	7	6	5	4	4	3	2 **Sandown**	

Apse Heath and Sandown 6d. Return.

CHILDREN'S FARES.

A child between 3-14 years of age half fare for single journey and single adult fare for a return journey.

I.W. COUNTY PRESS—1438-9-50

Wavell's Enterprise Bus Service: Newport to Sandown, 25th September 1950 until further notice

APPENDIX 3 – SALES OF INDEPENDENT OPERATORS' ROUTE LICENCES (1927 – 1956)

Firms' licences sold to Southern Vectis

1. B.H. Bullock (Surprise), Havenstreet (*Newport-Havenstreet-Binstead-Ryde*) plus 5 buses. 14.9.1929

2. F.W. Casey, Ryde (*Newport-Wootton Bridge-Ryde*) plus 3 buses 11.1929

3. A.H. Creeth and Sons (Premier), Nettlestone (*Ryde-Nettlestone-Seaview*) plus 6 vehicles 1.1.1930

4. I.W. Tourist Co. Ltd., Ryde (*Ryde-Seaview-St. Helens; Seaview-Shanklin*) plus 5 vehicles 19.6.1930

5. Hilton Dyer (Central), Godshill (*Newport-Godshill-Shanklin*) 4.6.1932

6. B.C.F. Bolwell (Regel), Lake (*Shanklin-Wroxall-Ventnor*) 1.7.1933

7. Hayles and Vanner (Supreme), Ryde (*Newport-Havenstreet-Haylands-Ryde*) plus 2 buses 1.7.1933

8. A.E. King, Carisbrooke (*Newport-Camp Hill and Newport-Whitecroft Hospital*) 25.3.1934

9. Andrew L. Morris, Ventnor (*Ventnor-Lowtherville*) 1.5.1934

10. Brown's Bus Service, Carisbrooke (*Newport-Shalfleet-Yarmouth-Totland Bay-Freshwater Bay; Newport-Calbourne-Yarmouth; Totland Bay-Alum Bay*) plus 12 buses 1.3.1935

11. Herbert Wheeler (*Newtown-Porchfield-Newport*) 1935

12. R. Walkden Ltd., Sandown (*Shanklin-Sandown-Ryde; Sandown-Newport; Sandown-Bembridge*) plus 8 buses 19.3.1936

13. C.A.G. Coffen (Pioneer Bus Service), Ryde (*Ryde-Elmfield; Ryde-Haylands; Ryde-Mersley Down summer service*) plus 6 buses 1.3.1937

14. Colson Brothers, Carisbrooke (*Newport-Carisbrooke-Gunville*) plus 4 buses 2.3.1939

15. M.J. Wavell (Enterprise Bus Service) (*Two Newport to Sandown routes via Blackwater, Arreton or Downend, Arreton and Newchurch*) plus 6 buses 18.6.1951

16. West Wight Motor Bus Co. Ltd., Freshwater (*Freshwater Bay- Yarmouth; Freshwater Bay-Alum Bay; Alum Bay-Yarmouth*) 16.6.1952

17. Bartletts' Coaches Ltd., Shanklin (*Luccombe-Shanklin*) 30.4.1956

18. Shotters' Ltd., Brighstone (*Newport-Brighstone-Compton Bay; Newport-Carisbrooke-Gunville*) 14.5.1956

19. Nash's Luxury Coaches, Ltd., Ventnor (*Ventnor Town service*) 1.6.1956

Firms' licences sold to other Isle of Wight bus operators

1. William E. Sprake (The Chale Favourite), Chale Green (*Chale-Niton-Whitwell-Ventnor*) to A.L. Morris c.1927

2. Brown's Bus Service, Carisbrooke (*Newtown-Porchfield-Newport*) to H.E.J. Wheeler, Porchfield 1929

3. Louis James Dallimore, Bembridge (*Bembridge - Sandown*) to R. Walkden Ltd., Sandown c.1930

4. A.H. Hunter (Pioneer Bus Service), Ryde (*Ryde-Haylands; Ryde-Elmfield*) plus several buses to C.A.G. Coffen, Ryde (Pioneer Bus Service) 1931

5. Mrs. M. Brown (Brown's Bus), Ventnor (*Ventnor Town service*) to G.K. Nash (Nash's Luxury Coaches Ltd.), Ventnor by 1937

6. Hilton Herbert Hall (West Wight Bus Service), Freshwater (*Freshwater-Newport*) to Brown's Bus Service, Carisbrooke 1931

7. F.D. Lawson (Regel Bus Service), Shanklin (*two routes Sandown to Bembridge and Shanklin to Ventnor*) to B.C.F. Bolwell (Regel), Lake 1932

8. J.L. Summers (Reliance Bus Service), Newport (*Newport to Gunville*) to G.A. Shotter and Sons 1937

9. Cooper, Freshwater and Pink Brothers, Totland Bay merged to form West Wight Motor Bus Co. Ltd. 1946

10. Blake's Bus Service, Newport (*Newport-Downend-Newchurch-Sandown*) to Enterprise Bus Service 2/1951

APPENDIX 4 – ISLE OF WIGHT BUS MANUFACTURERS AND COACHBUILDERS

1. The Liquid Fuel Engineering Company (LIFU), the Columbine Works, East Cowes. This innovative firm produced approximately 100 steam-powered lorries, vans, buses and charabancs between 1895 and 1900 before relocating to Poole.

2. George Mulliss and Company, Nelson Street, Ryde. Mulliss built seven 30-seat bodies for Milnes-Daimler single deck charabancs for Isle of Wight Express Motor Syndicate Ltd. in 1906. The coachbuilding firm continued to trade until the 1950s.

3. Arthur Herbert Creeth and Sons, Nettlestone. Creeths, a family of highly skilled blacksmiths, produced and repaired around ten single deck and double deck bodies for buses and charabancs that they operated between Ryde and Seaview between 1909 and 1930 (trading as Premier Motor Service).

4. F. Sivell, Ventnor. Sivell is known to have built one 29-seat charabanc body on a Daimler W chassis which was operated by E.H. Crinage from 1921 (DL 1827). (See photo in chapter 9)

5. Harry Margham and Sons Ltd., Crocker Street, Newport. This major firm manufactured approximately 30 bus, charabanc and coach bodies, rebodied at least 20 buses and repaired many PSVs between 1921 and 1949. (See chapter 8)

6. Harry Midlane, Coachbuilder and Painter, Albert Street, Newport. Midlane is believed to have constructed a 15-seat charabanc body for an imported Oldsmobile vehicle (DL 5039) in 1927.

This is the only known photograph of the only known charabanc body to be built by Harry Midlane of Newport. It was fitted to an Oldsmobile chassis. DL 5039 is seen working for a Norfolk operator in Cromer.

REFERENCES

Barham, Fisher (1979) Torbay Transport (Glasney Press)

Benest, Miss C.D.H., Personal scrapbook, 1905 – 1911

Creeth, Lilian (1991), *Steam Dreams: The story of an Isle of Wight family called Creeth* (author)

Cummings, John (1980), *Railway motor buses and bus services in the British Isles 1902 – 1933, Vol. 2* (Oxford Publishing Company)

Green, F.H.W. (1958), "Isle of Wight Services, thirty years on", *Buses Illustrated, November 1958* (Ian Allan Publishing Ltd.)

Harley, Allan (1965), "The trial of steam", *Old Motor and Vintage Commercial, Vol. 3, No. 12, June 1965* (Old Motor Magazine Ltd.)

Holbrook, Edwin, Unpublished memoirs, c. 1953

Isle of Wight County Press (local newspapers from 1902 – 1988)

Isle of Wight Express Motor Syndicate article in The Commercial Motor, 31st May 1906

Kaye, David (1972), *Buses and Trolleybuses before 1919* (Blandford Press Ltd.)

LIFU, East Cowes 1894 – 1900 (2008), (East Cowes Heritage Centre)

Morris, Colin (1980), *The history of British bus services: South East England* (Transport Publishing Company)

Newman, Richard (1989), *Southern Vectis – The first sixty years* (Ensign Publications for Southern Vectis)

Norris, Peter (1954), "The LIFU steam bus", *Buses Illustrated January – March 1954* (Ian Allan Publishing Ltd.)

Sprake, Derek (1993), *Put out the flag: the story of Isle of Wight carriers 1860 - 1960* (Cross Publishing)

Vincent, Don and Roberts, Chris (2008), *Isle of Wight registrations in the original DL – series, DL 1 – DL 9999 (1903 – 1935), 2nd edition with 2010 supplement* (copies available from authors)

Vincent, Don (1994), *Seaview Services: An illustrated fleet history 1922 – 1994* (G & K Publications)

Woodhall, Noel and Heaton, Brian (2008), *Car numbers then and now* (Registrations Publications)

LIST OF PHOTOGRAPHERS

P. Brannon (by kind permission of The Isle of Wight County Press Ltd.): Back cover

F.N. Broderick (Ryde): 30, 70, 71, 77

Mark Chessell: 106, 129, 131/ **Anne Clearey (nee Hunter) collection**: 92

Alan Cross: 66 (lower), 68 (top and lower), 111, 113 (top), 114, 116, 117

Alan Cross/J.F. Higham collection: Front cover, 55, 126 (top)

Richard Flack collection: 29, 30, 70, 74

Nigel Flux collection: 84 (lower), 87 (lower), 93 (left), 100/ **Marcus Gaywood**: 101

John Golding collection: 22, 84 (top), 85 (top and lower), 87 (top), 89, 90, 91, 93 (right), 97/

June Holbrook collection: 53/ **W.R. Hogg** (Ryde): 74

Isle of Wight County Press/Margham family: 64

Isle of Wight Record Office: 5, 6, 7, 8, 10, 23, 36, 45, 47, 71, 75, 76, 78, 79, 81

V.C. Jones/Omnibus Society: 119 (top)/ **Mr A.H. Kirk** (Freshwater): 79

Joan Kirkby (nee Wavell) collection: 86, 115, 138

Letter Box Study Group: 35/ **Louis Levy**: 23

Robert F. Mack: 110/ **Roy Marshall/Omnibus Society**: 118

Millar & Lang Ltd.: 80/ **Mr Millman-Brown** (Shanklin): 33

Omnibus Society: 61, 63, 64, 66 (top), 67, 69, 94 (top), 96, 103, 108, 120, 126 (lower)

Carole Osgood (nee Hunter) collection: 59

Barry Price collection: 2, 49, 54, 56, 135, 136/ **Peter J. Relph**: 119 (lower)

Royal Mail: 128/ **Keith Shotter collection**: 94 (lower), 95, 102, 124 (lower)

Graham Squibb collection: 51/ **Don Vincent**: 11, 13, 16

Roger Warwick collection: 83, 88, 98, 99/ **Peter Yeomans/ Omnibus Society**: 125

All other photographs, timetables and tickets are from the author's collection